POTENTIAL
"unrealized ability"

To reach your potential,
you need to make the changes
it takes to grow and improve.

PURE PROFIT

DOUBLE YOUR NET PROFIT
IN JUST 90 DAYS

The Best Part...

Your Greatest Potential
For Improvement Lies In
These 7 Key Areas.

BOOKS BY JOE VERDE

- Pure Profit – Double Your Net In Just 90 Days

- How To Sell A Car & Close The Sale Today

- Earn Over $100,000 Selling Cars – Every Year

- 38 Hot Tips On Selling More Cars In Today's Market

- 4 Secrets Separate You From Your Competition In Sales!

- 10 Critical Skills Every Automotive Sales Manager Needs

- Manage Your Career In Sales – Goal Setting For Salespeople

- A Dealer's Guide To Recovery And Growth In Today's Market

PURE PROFIT
DOUBLE YOUR NET PROFIT
IN JUST 90 DAYS

Joe Verde

DOES SELLING MORE
EQUAL MORE NET PROFIT?

Maybe – maybe not...
It depends on how you sell more!

Too many Dealers and Managers work very hard trying to sell more units to increase their net profit and are disappointed when the statement barely shows a blip of improvement.

You may be looking in all the wrong places to make that happen. If your goal is to improve your net profit, you also need to take a look at some old habits.

My goal is to show you how and where to focus to...

DOUBLE YOUR NET PROFIT

...without spending any extra money
on marketing, advertising or additional staff.

JOE VERDE

GETS RESULTS FAST

 Joe Verde, President of Joe Verde Sales and Management Training, Inc. is the recognized leader in automotive dealer, management and sales training for over 30 years.

Joe believes training should accomplish one goal; get results for the client.

For that reason, JVSMT Inc. is known as the *go to company* in the car business for immediate sales results and long-term growth. That's also why Joe's company works with half of the largest dealer groups, half of the Top 500 dealers, and with thousands of other dealerships all across North America, helping them to continually reach new levels in sales and profits.

Joe and his team of trainers (who have over 30 years combined experience training for Joe) have spoken to most dealer 20 groups and other industry meetings, to over 25 NADA annual conventions, and they hold hundreds of Joe Verde workshops each year.

The company is exclusive to the auto industry and is the driving force in sales and management training, providing common sense solutions to the problems and opportunities salespeople, managers and dealerships experience daily in selling more, earning more profit and retaining customers for life.

Joe Verde pioneered online sales training in the car business in 2005 with the Joe Verde Training Network® (JVTN®).

From his 'Fast Start' courses for new hires, to his continuing education training curriculum, and with over 10 million training chapters taken by salespeople, managers and dealers, JVTN® is the most valuable in-house training resource in the automotive industry today.

Why should you read this book and take Joe's solutions seriously? Because Joe Verde is the person who will help you get the results you're looking for.

Kathleen Rittmaster – General Manager

PURE PROFIT

DOUBLE YOUR NET PROFIT IN JUST 90 DAYS

Your Greatest Potential
To Quickly Double Your Net Profit
Lies In These 7 Key Areas!

Table Of Contents

*Follow these directions and
you'll increase your income for life.*

> # $7,096,980
> The realistic gross profit potential
> every year in a 100 unit dealership.

What is one extra sale worth?

That depends ... and that's what this book is all about. Because most of us were taught so many things about how to increase sales that actually prevent us from reaching those goals, we'll look at 7 quick and easy ways you can double your net profit in just 90 days that no one has pointed out to you before.

I promise – there aren't any gimmicks or off the wall ideas in this book. These are just common sense steps you can implement immediately to sell more units the right way – with no additional marketing expense per unit. That means you'll increase your net profit with each sale.

Looking For Profit In All The Wrong Places

While I was waiting to talk to a GM one day about training, I overheard him tell his manager the goal for the month. The very first thing his manager asked was, "So what's the budget?"

I understand why he asked the question because for my first five years in the car business, I was led to believe that everything about selling more had to do with price, and advertising, and negotiating a 'deal'.

We had no training on how to sell, so everything defaulted to price. We pre-qualified everyone on down, payments, trade, payoff and how soon they planned to buy, gave only a select few a decent demo and presentation, and closed with, "If we could get you a deal today, would you take it?"

We didn't have any real sales processes to follow, doing demos was optional, and our only goal was to get them inside and hope we could piece a deal together. We didn't learn to handle incoming calls, we never called someone back who didn't buy, prospecting was never on our 'to do' list, and retention – no thanks, just sell 'em and forget 'em.

Our managers didn't train us or manage us. They wrote ads, worked deals, appraised trades, ordered cars and did dealer trades. When it was slow, they complained about not being able to find good salespeople.

Everything I was taught then, and what most dealers and managers in class agree they're still doing, does *the opposite* of generating higher net profits.

Back to the question – what's one extra sale worth?

Ads: One sale, one time ... We'll get into this more, but when you buy a sale through advertising or when you buy a lead ... *you're buying just that one $2,500 sale, just one time.* There isn't another sale coming next month or next year from the money you just spent to bring in that sale.

Improvements: One sale, many times ... When you improve something though, whether it's a salesperson's skills, a selling process, or a manager's skills – that improvement generates multiple $2,500 sales. In fact, *as long as you maintain* the skills, or the process or whatever your manager learned to do differently to make more sales – those improvements will continue to generate those extra sales for years to come.

Short-Term Thinking vs. Long-Term Planning

80% of most dealerships' sales are those ad-driven, one shot deals. But when sales come from improvements that you maintain, one sale and $2,500 becomes 12 sales and $30,000 this year, and 120 sales and $300,000 in the next 10 years. Even better, if it's a one sale improvement by 10 salespeople, then it's a 10 unit and $25,000 improvement per month, 120 units and $300,000 per year, and 1,200 units and $3,000,000 in the next 10 years.

The real secret to growth and profit is simple: a) improve and sell more, b) stabilize and maintain that new level, c) improve and sell more, d) stabilize and maintain that new level, and keep repeating the process.

Sell More – Net More – Save More

If you combine your current sales and gross with the directions I'll cover in here, you will double your net profit. And no, you don't have to use our training to get all of these benefits.

It's also true that we're #1 in sales training for a reason, so if you do use us, you'll sell more, you'll increase your net profit *faster* and *save* even more money by *training* your managers and salespeople.

Go slow and really think about every solution we cover – because each offers *immediate improvements* that become lasting changes in your dealership to continually produce more sales, good gross, and higher net profits.

Grab a notebook to take notes and let's talk about how you can increase your unit sales, your good gross and your net profit overnight.

When you see this ✍, it's just to let you know that it's important to take notes, circle something or fill in the blanks.

Atlantic Auto Group

"The Joe Verde sales training is the single most important thing we do here.

Our entire sales staff from BDC reps. to General Managers go through this training program a few times a year. In addition we are all required to complete the Joe Verde online training that is offered.

The results speak for themselves. We have received a 14% increase in new car volume vs. 2013, while at the same time having a nice lift in gross profit.

We consider it the cornerstone to our success. It's one thing we refuse to do without."

– Michael Brown

YOUR CUSTOMERS
TODAY

On the next page, let's look at
the facts about your customers today.

To make the math in each solution easy to follow,
we'll use this sample 100 unit dealership in every example.

Sample 100 Unit Dealership
We'll Use For All Examples

Units Per Month 100

Closing / Delivery Ratio 20%

Average Gross Per Unit $2,500

Average Sales & Management Comp. 40%

Annual (Pre-Tax) Net Profit $500,000

WHICH OF THESE FACTS
AFFECT YOUR PAYCHECK?

✍ *Circle the # for each fact that affects your paycheck...*

1. 95%+ have done their research online and know what they want.

2. Customers today only stop in 2 dealerships before they buy.

3. 8 out of 10 people (78%) who walk on your lot in today's market came to buy, and 90% of them buy within a week.

4. 20% is the average closing ratio (2 of the 10).

5. 71% of customers buy because they like their salesperson.

6. 71% who didn't buy, found a vehicle in inventory they liked, but didn't like the salesperson, management or the process.

7. 86% overall, and 71% of internet shoppers didn't buy what they planned to buy; different color, equipment, model or brand.

8. 80% of their decision to purchase takes place in the demo and presentation, on just 20% of the features – their Hot Buttons.

9. 50% do buy on the spot when they get a 'Targeted' Presentation & 'Targeted' Demo on their key 'Hot Buttons'.

10. Price did not make it into the 'Top 10' when JD Powers most recently surveyed buyer concerns about purchasing a vehicle.

11. Gross is 40% higher with 'Targeted' Presentations and 'Targeted' Demos that focus on customer 'Hot Buttons', not price.

12. Gross is 40% higher with repeat, referral and dealership customers.

13. 16% of customers pay full price and 30% pay what they're asked to pay. (Too bad more weren't asked to pay full price.)

14. 8 out of 10 service customers would consider buying from you.

15. 30% of your service customers and customers in your 'sold' database have a family member who'll be buying within 90 days.

16. The average family will purchase a total of 36 vehicles, lifetime.

17. 90% of deliveries are never contacted again *about purchasing another vehicle* (perfect 10 & other automated letters don't count).

Highlight the most important facts to you.

How $750,000 Is Lost
From Floor Traffic Every Month

Dealerships aren't missing sales from a lack of opportunity. There is enough opportunity with the floor traffic dealers have on the lot each month now for them to double sales – *and then to double sales again.*

*Here's the math on what happens
in a 100 unit dealership that closes/delivers 20%.*

**The number of buyers on the lot
and the potential gross profit each month...**

500	People were on the lot each month
400	**Came to buy (8 of 10) and will buy somewhere**
x $2,500	The average gross profit per unit

$1,000,000

**In potential gross profit
walks onto your lot each month**

And then...

100	Purchase now for $250,000 in gross profit
300	**Buyers leave without buying (3 out of 4)**
x $2,500	Gross per unit on each *buyer* you don't sell

– $750,000

**In potential gross profit also
walks back off the lot each month**

*How can you get more of that $750,000?
We'll take a look at 7 different ways to do that.*

Buyers <u>Per 100 People</u> On The Lot

20 Buyers Are Delivered...

But 60 Other Buyers Leave & Are Still Available...

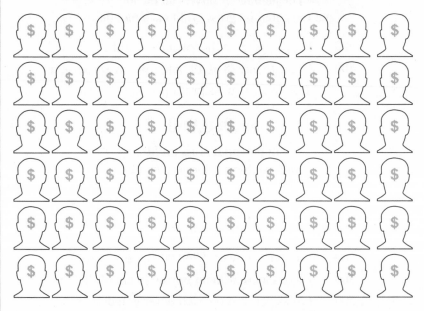

Only 20 People Can't Buy Or Don't Buy...

*A lack of floor traffic isn't the problem and
more floor traffic isn't the solution!*

✍ **Write Out Your Thoughts**

_____

_____

_____

_____

_____

_____

_____

_____

_____

_____

_____

_____

_____

_____

_____

_____

_____

_____

_____

_____

_____

_____

Thinking is the hardest thing for most people to do.

When you remember how to daydream with a purpose and discipline yourself to make the time regularly – you can accomplish anything.

Seriously – Slow Down

Take at least 20 minutes to really think about each of these 7 opportunities you have to improve your units, gross profit, and your net profit to find your best solution.

Tip: No TV, no kids, no calls, no texts, no emails. Just you, this book and a spiral notebook.

Yes, you really do have 20 minutes before your world will fall apart...

30 minutes though,
that's iffy, so be careful :)

To double your net, every dealer and manager needs to understand that there are two kinds of Gross Profit...

GOOD GROSS

&

BAD GROSS

Focus on *good gross* and you can easily...

• Double your net profit within 3-6 months

• Lower your 'cost per sale' across the board

• Increase your growth and profits year after year

WHAT IS GOOD GROSS?

Good Gross comes from *improving* sales or gross, *without adding any extra expenses.* When you don't add additional expenses to generate a another sale and gross profit ... the only expense to that extra sale and gross is your sales and management compensation of +/– 40%.

60% Of Good Gross Becomes Net Profit

Here are 5 *easy ways to* generate more good gross...

- Sell more to traffic you already have. A 100 unit dealership has already paid for the 500 people on the lot and delivers 20% (100). Sell 10 more of those 500 and there's no extra expense. That extra $25,000 gross also becomes $15,000 in net profit. Added benefit – lower overall cost per sale.

- Raise the gross ... There's no extra expense when salespeople sell value instead of price. Raise the gross $250 on 100 units, and you've picked up $25,000 more with no new expense except your sales and management compensation of about 40%. The rest, $15,000, is pure profit.

- Get more 'missed' sales back in with better Unsold Follow Up ... Put just one more be-back a day on the lot (30 total), deliver (67%) = 20 more units for $50,000 gross and $30,000 net. Again, no new expense because you already paid to get them to show up the first time.

- 100 unit dealerships get 250 +/– incoming sales calls and leads a month. Improve your 'appointment show' ratio (without a BDC) and generate more good gross. 20+ extra units is easy in a 100 unit store – and add on another $50,000 gross & $30,000 net.

- Repeat Customers – Service Customers – Easy Referrals ... are all low cost, easy to sell customers for good gross. Even better, you save $400 in 'cost per sale', plus these sources *generate 40% higher gross profits* for *even more* Good Gross & Net Profit. Sales to these groups cost $400 less, generate $800 more per unit in gross, and are 'Pure Profit' compared to 'walk in' traffic.

Good Gross Generates Net Profit

There's $100,000+ (above) in net profit <u>every month,</u> if you focus on the right areas – plus everything has already been expensed so that other than sales and management compensation, about 60% of the extra gross becomes profit.

You are sitting on a Gold Mine – and doubling your net is right around the corner when you focus on these 'no extra expense' selling opportunities.

WHAT IS BAD GROSS?

Bad Gross comes from adding extra expenses to increase sales. Why? Because the additional expense overrides most of the benefit.

I'm definitely *not saying* 'don't do this' – but every example below can cost you most or all of the benefit of the extra sales and gross.

- Events ... That 100 unit dealership puts on a big weekend extravaganza.

  Total Investment $20,000

  Total Weekend Sales ....32 Units (12 avg. + 20 from the event)

  Extra Weekend Gross........$50,000 ($2,500 x 20 extra units)

  End of Month Totals........120 units & $300,000 Total Gross

  Awesome! They're up 20 units and $50,000. High-fives everywhere!

  So let's go over the math real quick on this event...

	$ 50,000	Total Gross (20 Units)
–	$ 20,000	Cost of the event
–	$ 20,000	40% Sales & Management Comp.
–	$ 1,000	Or more for bonuses – 'Hat Tricks', etc.
–	$ 2,000	Issues: Trades / rewrites / unwinds, etc.
	$ 7,000	Balance before any other surprises

- Buying Leads ... In a 100 unit dealership with a $500 cost PVR now, when they buy 20 more $500 leads ($10,000) even if they all become deliveries, most of those deals are absorbed into the 100 units they were already delivering, but their new cost per sale is $600.

- Advertising ... As a new dealership, ads are important to build your business. But in an industry where *everybody* continues to buy the product, after a couple years, a new dealership should have enough sold customers, service customers and referrals to cut their advertising by 80% and still grow every year from repeat and referral business.

  Advertising is a 'one-trick pony' on a merry-go-round in the house of smoke & mirrors. You know that only half of your ads work, but you're not sure which half because it's so hard to track. Advertising is so addictive, dealers start to believe they can't live without it.

  ROI: Advertising to drive traffic ... $2 in return for $1 invested.

  ROI: Training to sell the traffic you have ... $30 for every $1 invested.

COMMON BAD GROSS PROBLEMS

After my presentation on Phone Rooms & BDCs at the NADA Convention, Robert, a dealer asked a question I've heard dozens of times...

> *"We sell 100 units, I added a BDC and track 40 units to it each month, but I'm still only selling 100 units – what happened?"*

Like most dealers, Robert installed a phone room because his salespeople focused on price, talked too much, didn't set appointments, the appointments they set didn't show – and most of the sales they could have made, were lost.

But why aren't salespeople very good on the phones?

- No Selling Skills ... Phone skills <u>are not</u> a separate skill set, they're just selling skills a salesperson or manager uses when they pick up a phone.

  For instance, if you can't control a conversation *with questions* on the lot, if you can't *bypass price* on the lot, *deal with objections* or *close* on the lot, you can't close an appointment on the phone either.

  80% haven't been taught to sell so they can't handle calls correctly either.

- No Management On Handling Phones ... Managers weren't trained on the core selling skills either, and when promoted weren't taught how to train, coach and manage salespeople daily, much less manage processes like handling incoming calls, prospecting or long-term retention.

  Phone leads require selling skills, a clear process, and daily management.

So instead of training his salespeople and managers ... Robert hired another whole team to do their job instead, hoping that would solve his problem.

- Oops, new problem ... Now his average and below average salespeople are getting high-value prospects every day who close at 40-60% instead of the 10-20% for the walk-ins they'd been relying on. Now they can still sell the same number of units, with even less effort.

Really Bad Gross ... No rocket science needed – hiring two groups to do one task because the first group can't or won't, generates *extremely bad gross*. While there is a correct way to set up and use a BDC effectively, this isn't it.

Good Gross Option ... Your higher achievers who average 20-30+ units do need help because they run out of time to do some of the small, but critical tasks on paperwork, deliveries, long term follow up, social media, verifying appointments, etc., and need some 'sales assistance' so they can sell even more.

1 or 2 assistants for your 20-30+ unit salespeople will generate more sales and net per year than a BDC, for less $ *per year* than a BDC costs *per month*.

Where is your focus now – Good Gross or Bad Gross?

✍ *List 3 things your dealership focuses on that generate **Good Gross**...*

1. _____

   Why does this generate good gross? _____

   _____

   How can we do more? _____

2. _____

   Why does this generate good gross? _____

   _____

   How can we do more? _____

3. _____

   Why does this generate good gross? _____

   _____

   How can we do more? _____

✍ *Now list 3 things you focus on regularly that generate **Bad Gross**...*

1. _____

   Why does this generate bad gross? _____

   _____

   What could we do instead?_____

2. _____

   Why does this generate bad gross? _____

   _____

   What could we do instead?_____

3. _____

   Why does this generate bad gross? _____

   _____

   What could we do instead?_____

"My units and gross improved 60%!"

"After selling cars for 5 years, I went to Joe's 2-Day Sales Course and realized I had been doing so many things wrong that I was lucky to have the business I did have.

After the workshop, I focused on building **value** and following **each step** of the sale. My units and gross per deal quickly improved by 60%.

I've since been promoted to Sales Manager and now I'm training my staff on JVTN® each day. My superiors couldn't be more pleased with our performance. Thanks Joe!"

— Craig Runshe, Sales Manager
Hubbard GM Center, Monticello, Indiana

✍ **Write Out Your Thoughts**

_____

_____

_____

_____

_____

_____

_____

_____

_____

_____

_____

_____

_____

_____

_____

_____

_____

_____

_____

_____

_____

_____

_____

_____

Take the time to think, so you can continue to grow.

Just find a quiet spot with no distractions and take a few minutes to daydream with a purpose. If you will, you can accomplish anything.

Seriously...
Stop Reading & Write Your Notes

Memories fade fast, especially when you rush through these solutions to doubling your net.

You wouldn't still be reading this if you weren't serious about improving, and there's just too much to consider in each solution to make this a quick read.

You'll get so much more out of this book and improve in each area faster, if you'll just take 20 minutes (or even the rest of the day) to really think about each of these opportunities.

Just jot down your ideas and add a short bullet point plan of action at the end of every chapter, so that you'll remember all the great ideas you come up with as you read through this book.

'A Trick Question'

What % of improvement
in units and gross do you need to...

Double Your Net Profit

✍ *Pick one before you keep reading...*

10% – 15% – 20% – 30% – 45% – 50%
60% – 75% – 80% – 95% – 100%

To make the math in each solution easy to follow,
we'll use this sample 100 unit dealership in every example.

Sample 100 Unit Dealership We'll Use For All Examples
Units Per Month..100
Closing / Delivery Ratio.....................................20%
Average Gross Per Unit................................. $2,500
Average Sales & Management Comp. 40%
Annual (Pre-Tax) Net Profit...................... $500,000

What % Of Increase Do You Think You Need In Units & Gross To Double Your Net Profit?

Your answer depends on whether you focus on generating *good gross* or *bad gross* – which we talked about in the last chapter...

So just go ahead and answer this question:

To double your net profit, what % of increase do you need in units and gross profit combined, when you improve using 'Good Gross' options?

✍ *Circle one before you keep reading:*
10% – 15% – 20% – 30% – 45% – 50%
60% – 75% – 80% – 95% – 100%

✍ What did you pick: 25% – 50% – 75%? or _____%

To double your net profit ...

If our sample 100 unit dealership focuses on 'Good Gross' sources, when they increase total *units sold by just 15 units,* from 100 to 115, and when they increase their *gross per unit just $375,* from $2,500 to $2,875, they'll double their net profit. Yes, that's <u>double net</u> – just from a 15% increase.

You just have to focus on 'Good Gross'...

Now	100 units @ $2,500 per = $250,000 per month
Improve 15%	115 units @ $2,875 per = $330,625 per month
	That's $80,625 more 'Good Gross' per month
	@ 60% to net, that's $48,375 in extra net per month
	That's **$580,500 more <u>net profit</u>** per year
<u>New</u> **Net Profit**	**$1,080,500** net per year ($500,000 + $580,500)

116% improvement in net profit just
from a 15% improvement in units and gross!
Why weren't all of us taught this simple formula?
(See the chart on the next page for more examples.)

This Is What You Can Accomplish In Net Profit
When You Learn To Focus On Creating 'Good Gross'

Units – Gross – Net NOW		% Unit & Gross Improvement					
		5.0%	10.0%	15.0%	20.0%	25.0%	50.0%
Monthly Units	100	105	110	115	120	125	150
Gross PVR	$2,500	$2,625	$2,750	$2,875	$3,000	$3,125	$3,750
Total Gross Per Month	$250,000						
Total Gross Per Year	$3,000,000						
Net Profit Per Year Now	$500,000						
New Results From Improvements		5.0%	10.0%	15.0%	20.0%	25.0%	50.0%
Gross Profit Per Month		$275,625	$302,500	$330,625	$360,000	$390,625	$562,500
Gross Profit Per Year		$3,307,500	$3,630,000	$3,967,500	$4,320,000	$4,687,500	$6,750,000
Additional New 'Good' Gross Per Month		$25,625	$52,500	$80,625	$110,000	$140,625	$312,500
Additional Net Profit / Mo. From 'Good' Gross		$15,375	$31,500	$48,375	$66,000	$84,375	$187,500
Additional Net Profit / Year From 'Good' Gross		$184,500	$378,000	$580,500	$792,000	$1,012,500	$2,250,000
New Annual Net Profit		$684,500	$878,000	$1,080,500	$1,292,000	$1,512,500	$2,750,000
% Improvement In Net Profit		37%	76%	116%	158%	203%	450%

Do more 'what if' math for your dealership.
Just use our calculators at JoeVerde.com/netcalc

Is a 15% improvement
in units and gross realistic?

"We started using Joe's online training 3 months ago, along with having weekly training meetings. We are focusing on using Joe's word tracks to **overcome objections** and making sure salespeople **do not skip any steps** in the sales process.

With just those minor changes, we had our **2nd best month in 10 years** and now are on track for our best year ever.

Thanks Joe!"

– Jake Sodikoff, General Manager
Steven Kia, Harrisonburg, Virginia

Jake's update,
5 months later...

"After 8 months training on JVTN® 3 days a week, our volume is up 16% over last year and our gross is already 20% higher than 2013.

In addition, we had a record month in September! JVTN® has helped our sales team **overcome objections** on the lot and has helped us **close deals** we never would have had."

– Jake Sodikoff, General Manager
Steven Kia, Harrisonburg, Virginia

7 WAYS YOU CAN DOUBLE YOUR NET PROFIT IN JUST 90 DAYS

(With the traffic you have now.)

To make the math in each solution easy to follow,
we'll use this sample 100 unit dealership in every example.

Sample 100 Unit Dealership
We'll Use For All Examples

Units Per Month 100

Closing / Delivery Ratio 20%

Average Gross Per Unit $2,500

Average Sales & Management Comp. 40%

Annual (Pre-Tax) Net Profit $500,000

If this is starting to make sense – get every manager involved!

1. You'll want every manager on board as you start setting your goals, so get every manager a copy of this short book.

2. Have every manager read it, add in your dealership numbers, do the math, set a quick goal and fill in an action plan in each area on what you want to improve.

3. Schedule management meetings to talk about each solution. Have everyone discuss their notes on the opportunity, their estimates of the potential to improve, and the steps they feel need to be taken to implement the plan.

4. As a group, select <u>one area to focus on for the next 90 days</u> (or until you reach that goal) and as a group, set a realistic goal.

   (Remember, my goal setting book is free: JoeVerde.com/store)

5. Work with your salespeople on that topic every day. It doesn't have to be an hour meeting – just get everyone *talking* about what they're doing, share their success and where they need more help.

6. Track everything involved in that particular activity. If it's making the sale – track total ups, demos, write ups (committed and non-committed), deliveries, gross, manager who worked the deal, and source it accurately.

7. At the end of every 30 days, review your progress, adapt and adjust your plan as needed, and focus on the next 30 days.

   Schedule your plans and training for 30 days at a time, and stay focused on that solution until you reach your goal.

On your training to reach your goals...

There's a good chance you're on JVTN® now, and that means *you have a complete training course for every topic in this book.* So just follow the directions in each course on the number of meetings to hold, discussion topics in each meeting, practice sessions, and easy spiffs to keep the focus on that activity.

Or if you've been through our sales class, or our closing and objection handling workshop for salespeople, or our desking and negotiation workshop for managers, use your workbooks as guides to move the needle in every area that is sales related.

FLOOR TRAFFIC
Solution #1

Improve The
Selling Process

Is doubling your unit sales possible?

I know that sounds impossible when you're working hard to sell what you're selling now. But think back to those first stats we covered or the chart of buyers – 8 out of 10 people who come into your dealership to look, do buy, and the average dealership delivers just 20% of their floor traffic (2 out of 10).

In reality, using those two stats or just looking at the chart of buyers, there are enough unsold buyers right now for that 100 unit dealership to deliver 400 units per month with no additional floor traffic.

You aren't going to sell everyone on your lot, we all know that. But when you have the potential to deliver 4 times as many vehicles as you are now, selling 20%-30%-50% or even 100% more just means improving your skills and processes.

More importantly, you can increase your sales volume, your gross and your net profit without spending any more money on more ads, marketing or leads.

WHICH OF THESE FACTS
AFFECT YOUR PAYCHECK?

The 3 Stage Selling Process Facts & Stats...
Warm Up – Build Value – Close

✎ Circle the # for each fact that affects your paycheck...

1. 95%+ of the people have done some research online.

2. 8 out of 10 people who come into the dealership will buy.

3. 71% buy because they like their salesperson and the process.

4. 71% who didn't buy, found a vehicle they would have purchased but didn't like the salesperson or the process.

5. 85% said their salesperson didn't build rapport.

6. 80% of buying & selling is on just 20% of the features (Hot Buttons).

7. 85% said their salesperson didn't find out what was important.

8. 88% said their presentation and demonstration were not targeted to their specific wants, needs and hot buttons.

9. Salespeople will get an average of 5 non-price buying objections they'll have to successfully overcome to deliver a vehicle.

10. 75% of salespeople only know 1 closing question / objection method - it's always price related, and 75% only ask 1 time.

11. Closing and the wrap up to start the paperwork is a 4-step process that begins at the very end of the demonstration.

12. Speed Kills Selling. Closing ratios are at 6% when salespeople spend less than 60 minutes on the lot with a customer, 31% at 72 minutes, and 57% when they spend 100 minutes or more.

13. The average delivery ratio from all sources is 20% (2 out of 10).

Why is it so easy to sell more?

Because 8 out of 10 came to buy and dealerships are only selling 20% – that's just 2 of the 8. How hard should it be to deliver 1 or 2 more to the 6 who only came to buy a vehicle?

HOW TO REALISTICALLY IMPROVE
SALES 50 UNITS & YOUR NET $900,000

Improve Your Selling Skills And Process

No need for unrealistic highballs ... just improve your actual closing ratio from 20% to 30% and you'll increase deliveries by 50%.

Sales Now – Closing At 20%		Improve Closing Ratio To 30%	
500	Prospects	500	Prospects
x 20%	Closing Ratio	x 30%	Closing Ratio
100	Deliveries	150	Deliveries

Your Good Gross Improvement

50	More units every month
x $2,500	Gross per unit
$125,000	Additional Good Gross per month

$1,500,000

Additional **Good Gross** per year

Your Net Profit Increase

x 60%	Good Gross to Net Profit
$75,000	Additional Net Profit per month

+ $900,000

Additional **Net Profit** per year

Your Cost To Increase Sales & Net Profit ... $1,270

SALESPEOPLE LACK CORE SKILLS

What Is Their Skill Level Now?

We've surveyed over 3,500 salespeople formally online, and thousands more informally in every class. Without exception, the average salesperson hasn't had enough training to even become average, much less to become successful. That's one reason 82% of new hires are back out of the business within 6 months and 80% of those who stay become *just average* or below.

• Fast Food Employees ... Offer a $1-$5 product. Workers earn around $9 to $10 per hour, get one to two weeks *plus* of 1-1 training initially with a team leader, and ongoing training and review the rest of their career.

• Automobile Salespeople ... Sell a $25,000-$100,000 product with unlimited variations in models, colors & equipment, who must handle an average of 5 non-price buying objections, and negotiate a win/win to deliver a vehicle.

Training: 7.4 hours of initial training – and 80% of that is on product, not on how to sell. They rated their initial training overall as a 4 out of 10 and there's no continuous *sales* training in 70% of the dealerships.

Average salespeople in the car business
deliver under 10 units and earn +/– $40,000 per year.

High achievers in automobile sales deliver 20 to 100+ units per month, and earn $100,000 to $400,000 per year. We work with them regularly, and have helped develop most of the highest achievers in our business.

The differences between average salespeople and those highest achievers boil down to 4 key areas that control everyone's success in sales. We refer to these in our classes as SHAC. They are...

• **Skills** ... Higher achievers obviously have higher skill levels in sales.

• **Habits** ... They go to work 'to work' and they spend their entire day doing something to sell now, or to generate a sale in the future.

• **Attitude** ... All high achievers have a positive attitude about selling and success and are successful because they expect to succeed.

• **Choice Of Customers** ... High achievers develop their own customer base and make most of their sales to repeat customers, service customers, referrals and prospects they bring into the dealership. They do not focus on the hard to close, price shopping walk-in customers dealers provide.

To improve, just make some part of SHAC your daily priority.

CORE SKILLS SALESPEOPLE NEED

A Common Misunderstanding On
Processes vs. Skills

Processes ... A process is made up of steps you take to complete something, whether it's building a house, selling a car, or prospecting out in service.

Common processes your salespeople need...

- How to sell the vehicle
- How to take an incoming call
- How to prospect for new business
- How to follow up & get unsold customers back in who just left
- How to follow up sold customers immediately
- And more, because everything you want or need salespeople to do is process based. That's why having effective processes is critical.

Every process above is different because there is a different goal in each. The *8 Steps To Selling A Car* are different than the *6 Steps To Turning A Call Into An Appointment,* which is different than the *3 Steps To Prospecting* to find the next driver in the family.

Here's where the confusion is on processes and skills...

3 Core Selling Skills ... The steps in each process are different, but the core skills required for each process **are the same** and fall into 3 main categories (below). That's why you'll hear me say, *"Phone skills are not a different set of skills, they're just selling skills you use when you have a phone in your hand."*

- **Asking Questions** is a critical core skill in every process above.

- **Dealing With Price** on the lot, when closing, in the negotiation, in taking calls, doing follow up and responding to leads is another core skill.

- **Selling Skills** like closing, building value, overcoming objections, and negotiating are critical skills salespeople need in every process.

To use incoming calls for example ... If a salesperson can't ask the *right questions* to control the conversation and get information on the lot, they can't on the phone either. If they can't *handle price* effectively on the lot, they can't on the phone. And if they can't *sell* to build value, overcome objections and close the sale on the lot, they sure can't sell, overcome objections or close on an appointment on the phone either.

The success you want most comes from skills your salespeople lack.

Rate Each Salesperson's Selling Skills (1-10) ✎ List salespeople, score each area, then find 'average'.

30 Ways To Improve Sales & Gross Rate Every Salesperson In Each Area From 1-10 *Do they do it at all – and what's their skill level?*													Totals	Average
QUESTIONS														
1. 'Yes' Questions: Ties Down Benefits / Commitments														
2. Open Ended Questions: Builds Rapport														
3. 'Either / Or' Questions: Controls – Investigates – Closes														
PRICE: QUESTIONS – CONCERNS – OBJECTIONS														
4. Bypasses Price On Lot & Focuses On Value														
5. Rephrases Price When Closing														
6. Refocuses Price In Negotiation														
SELLING PROCESS														
7. Correct Greeting To Get Name & Control														
8. Builds Rapport														
9. Investigates To Find Customer HOT BUTTONS														
10. Service: Sells People & Value														
11. Control: Keeps The Sale Moving Forward														
12. Selects Best Vehicle On HOT BUTTONS – Not Price														
13. Demo: Salesperson Drives 1st > Covers FABs														
14. Targeted Pres. & Demo To Secondary > Primary Driver														
15. Starts Closing Now With 5 to 7 Summary 'Yes' Questions														
16. Assumptive 'Sold Line' & 'Either / Or' Closing Question														
17. Gets 6 To 12 Action Closing Commitments														
18. Silent Trade Walk Around W/MPG & Maintenance Info														
19. Wrap Up & Final 'Either / Or' Close To Move Inside														
20. Negotiation: Properly Sets Up & Gets First Signature														
21. Completes Req. Paperwork B4 Negotiation Starts														
22. Gets Committed Buyers On All Write Ups														
23. Negotiation: Rate 3-Pass Process, Overall...														
24. Works Terms (Down & Payment) Not Price														
25. Maintains Control In The Negotiation														
26. Effective W/Gas Saving & Maintenance Closes														
27. Effectively & Correctly Transitions To Finance														
CLOSING ON OBJECTIONS														
28. Uses 'Seriously Now' In Closing & Negotiation														
29. Uses 'Agree & Close' In Closing & Negotiation														
30. Uses CRIC: Clarify – Rephrase – Isolate – Close														
Total Scores														

These Selling Skills Control All 7 Areas
You Want To Improve To Double Your Net Profit

✍ Write out your thoughts now – it's important.
And if you didn't actually ✍ a rating – stop and do that first.

_____

_____

_____

_____

_____

_____

_____

_____

_____

_____

_____

_____

_____

_____

_____

_____

_____

_____

_____

_____

"Luck is what happens when preparation meets opportunity."
– Seneca / Circa: 65 AD

SELLING SKILLS POTENTIAL

The Potential Good Gross Improvement You See

1.   ✐ Complete the Rating Sheet, then list all of your salespeople who could sell more by improving their selling skills and write in what you see as a realistic improvement for that salesperson.

_____ by + ___units   _____ by + ___units

_____ by + ___units   _____ by + ___units

_____ by + ___units   _____ by + ___units

_____ by + ___units   _____ by + ___units

_____ by + ___units   _____ by + ___units

_____ by + ___units   _____ by + ___units

_____ by + ___units   _____ by + ___units

_____ by + ___units   _____ by + ___units

Total improvement from every salesperson...   + _____ Units

2.   ✐ **The Math:** If your salespeople improved their core selling skills...

a. From #1, we could realistically sell   _____ **more units per mo.**

b. Using our total sales and F&I gross of $_____ per unit

c. 'a' x 'b' would add *good gross* of $_____,_____ per mo.

d. At 60% of 'c' to net, we'd *net an extra* $_____,_____ per mo.

e. In one year, that extra net profit would be $___ , _____ , _____

3.   ✐ **WIIFM** (What's in it for me?) If we did a better job of selling and delivered those extra units every month...

I'd personally earn an extra $ _____ per month,

and that means I'd make $ _____ more per year.

SELLING SKILLS

My Action Page & 90 Day Goal

1. Tip: Have every manager rate the same salespeople, then compare notes, so all managers are on the same page about what needs to be done to start improving right away.

2. ✍ My 90 day goal: We'll improve our *90 day unit sales average* from _____ units per month to _____ units per month by ___ / ___ / ___.
   (Read my book, "Goal Setting For Salespeople" to see how to work with current averages instead of month to month sales, especially when you're working to improve your average. It's free.)

3. ✍ The steps we'll take to reach our goals are...

   1. _____
      _____

   2. _____
      _____

   3. _____
      _____

   4. _____
      _____

   ✓ Tip: Create a 'goals' book for yourself. A simple spiral notebook or 3 ring binder works great.
   ✓ Tip: Get my book, "Goal Setting For Salespeople" for every salesperson and manager. Go to joeverde.com/store. It's free.
   ✓ Tip: Give each manager a small group of salespeople to train, coach and manage to help each salesperson achieve their individual goals.

4. To improve sales, gross, and profit...hold a short management meeting each morning on your progress until you reach your goal.

"Sales are missed by a few words – not by a few dollars." – Joe Verde

✍ **Write Out Your Thoughts**

_____

_____

_____

_____

_____

_____

_____

_____

_____

_____

_____

_____

_____

_____

_____

_____

_____

_____

_____

_____

_____

_____

_____

_____

Thinking is the hardest thing for most people to do.

When you remember how to daydream with a purpose and discipline
yourself to make the time regularly – you can accomplish anything.

"I feel like a kid in a candy store!"

We were covering these solutions in class and a manager said, "I feel like a kid in a candy store, and I can't wait to get started!"

If you feel that way, too, then it's even more important to slow down long enough to take really good notes and list what you feel is your potential.

To make it happen, compare notes with the other managers in your next management meeting, so you can all focus on the same solution at the same time, with the same plan of attack.

"From 5 units to 17 and double commissions with JVTN®."

"I have been in the car business for 6 months. Prior to this, I was in the restaurant business and working a lot of hours for not a lot of pay.

I've been training on JVTN® since Day 1. My first month, I sold 5 and my commission average was $300 per unit. Now 5 months later by following **Joe's basics**, mastering **CRIC** and overcoming objections, I am at 17 cars and have **doubled my commission** to $600 per unit!

I have truly found a profession that has given me untapped potential for all the effort I put forth! Thanks Joe!"

– Michael Wilson, Salesperson
Sierra Blanca Motors, Ruidoso, New Mexico

$400,000 Per Year Increase!

More Skills = More Sales
Both of these salespeople increased the 'good gross'
in each of their dealerships by over $400,000 per year
from improving their Core Selling Skills.

"From 6.5 to 20 units per month with Joe's training!"

"I have been in the car business for 5 months and thanks to Joe Verde and JVTN®, I am the top salesperson in my store!

Having never sold a car before, I was so lucky to be at a dealership that offered real training. I have been training on JVTN® regularly and after recently attending Joe's 2-Day Sales Workshop, it all came together.

I went from selling 6.5 cars, to 15 cars, then to 20. My gross has been getting better with every vehicle I sell. I've learned how to stay off **price** with Joe's 3-step process, build more **value** with his **steps to the sale**, and most importantly, to stay out of the huddle.

I love JVTN® because it gets me in the right attitude that they are all buyers! It also gives me the 'How-To's' to become a professional in sales and earn $100K. Thanks Joe!"

– Lance Horner, Salesperson
Brinson Ford-Lincoln, Athens, Texas

FLOOR TRAFFIC
SOLUTION #2

MORE DEMOS – MEAN – MORE SALES

Most salespeople want to jump on the fast track to the sale and get it over with quick, so they can get another 'up', especially on those busy traffic days.

To save time, one of the most common shortcuts salespeople take is to skip the demonstration and just try to get 'em inside as quickly as possible.

The problem with that, and one of the biggest reasons dealerships miss some easy sales is because...

NO DEMO – MEANS – NO SALE

Please note ... This solution is only about increasing the quantity of demos – not the quality.

Keep in mind ... we aren't talking about improving your salespeople's skills or your current demo process. We're just talking about increasing the *number of demos* given in your dealership each month.

Of course a great demo is better, but even your worst salesperson will deliver more units if they just put more people behind the wheel.

WHICH OF THESE FACTS
AFFECT YOUR PAYCHECK?

✍ *Circle the # for each fact that affects your paycheck...*

1. 99% of the people will not buy without driving first.

2. 80% of buying and selling happens in the demonstration and presentation steps on just 20% of their Hot Button features.

3. Buying is 'Emotional' and the demonstration is the highest emotional point in the selling process.

4. The targeted presentations to the secondary driver and then to the primary driver *set up the 4-step closing sequence.*

5. 50% who get a good demonstration buy on the spot.

6. But ... only 40% get a demo. In all of our classes and from our online survey of 3,500+, salespeople and managers admit they only give 4 out of 10 of your *(expensive)* prospects a demo.

   Why are their numbers different than your log sheets? Because we ask, "Forget what you put on the log sheet, in real life, how many out of every 10 people you talk to on the lot, including service customers who come up front, people on their lunch hour and even kids who tell you their parents told them to start looking, actually get a demonstration?"

   (4) is always the average. Why count service, lunch hour lookers and kids? Because we've all delivered some of them in the past, but not until they got a good demo and presentation. Count everyone!

   Some dealers say, "We're doing 75% demos."

So far, I've never found even one dealership (that counted everyone who shows an interest in a vehicle) with a real 75% demo rate. Some argued they did, *until they hired a spotter* to count everyone their salespeople talk to. It's always been closer to 40% than 75%.

More demos equal more sales because...

With an average 20% closing ratio and knowing 50% purchase after they get a demonstration, do your own math and you'll find you're currently delivering half the people who are getting demos now.

How To Realistically Improve
Sales 50 Units & Your Net $900,000

Increase Demos & Deliver More Vehicles

No unrealistic highballs here either ... just demo 6 instead of 4.

Sales by demo ratio now...   *After your improvement...*

Now – At 40% Demos		Improve Demo Ratio To 60%	
500	Prospects	500	Prospects
x 40%	Demos	x 60%	Demos
200	Demos →	300	Demos
x 50%	Buy w/good Demo	x 50%	Buy w/good Demo
100	Deliveries →	150	Deliveries

Your Good Gross Improvement

50	More units every month
x $2,500	More in Good Gross per unit
$125,000	Additional Good Gross per month

$1,500,000

Additional **Good Gross** per year

Your Net Profit Increase

x 60%	Good Gross to Net Profit
$75,000	Additional Net Profit per month

+ $900,000

Additional **Net Profit** per year

Your Cost To Increase Sales & Net Profit ... $1,270

Double down on demos and you'll double up on sales!

OUR DEMO POTENTIAL

The Potential You See In Your Dealership

1. ✍ As a dealership, how are you doing on demonstrating the vehicle to every customer now? Rate your dealership from 10% - 100%.

    10% – 20 – 30 – 40 – 50 – 60 – 70 – 80 – 90 – 100%

    Wait! Most managers in class start to use the numbers posted on their log sheet, but they know those numbers aren't accurate. We're talking real life for this rating, with no fluff.

    Counting service customers who look at a vehicle, those 'just looking' customers, and even kids who say they need someone else for approval, how many out of 10 are getting a demonstration?

    Be brutally honest in your guesstimate so you can set a real improvement goal. Circle your real percentage of demos now.

    Tip: If you aren't sure on demos, just take your sales volume and double it, and that's about how many demos salespeople are doing.

    ✍ If we just got more people behind the wheel of our vehicles each month, **I believe we could sell _____ more units every month.**

2. ✍ **The Math:** If we just did more demos...

    a. From #1, we could realistically sell   _____ **more units per mo.**

    b. Using our total sales and F&I gross of $_____ per unit

    c. 'a' x 'b' would add *good gross* of $_____,_____ per mo.

    d. At 60% of 'c' to net, we'd *net an extra* $_____,_____ per mo.

    e. In one year, that extra net profit would be $___ , _____ , _____

3. ✍ **WIIFM** (What's in it for me?) If we did more demos and sold those extra units every month...

    I'd personally earn an extra $ _____ per month,
    and that means I'd make $ _____ more per year.

    Double down on demos – and you'll double up on sales!

DEMO IMPROVEMENT

My Action Page & 90 Day Goal

1. ✍ List your salespeople who could improve their demo ratio. Fill in the number of units they're at now and then write in their realistic potential by improving their # of demos. How many more deliveries that would mean per month...

Salesperson	Units Now	Improve # Demos	Extra Units
_____	_____ units	_____ %	_____ Mo.
_____	_____ units	_____ %	_____ Mo.
_____	_____ units	_____ %	_____ Mo.
_____	_____ units	_____ %	_____ Mo.
_____	_____ units	_____ %	_____ Mo.
_____	_____ units	_____ %	_____ Mo.
_____	_____ units	_____ %	_____ Mo.
_____	_____ units	_____ %	_____ Mo.
_____	_____ units	_____ %	_____ Mo.
_____	_____ units	_____ %	_____ Mo.
_____	_____ units	_____ %	_____ Mo.
_____	_____ units	_____ %	_____ Mo.

Total Extra Units For The Dealership...   _____ **Mo.**

2. What are some things you can do to increase your number of demos?

    • **WIIFT** ... Talk to salespeople about *'what's in it for them'* to do more demos – more sales, easy sales, more income, more fun.

    • Train on how to get more customers behind the wheel.

    • Train on how to do more effective demonstrations that 'sell'.

    • Create easy spiffs that tie to the activity you want: more demos.

    Tip: If you're on JVTN® - go through the course, "How To Sell More Cars Every Month" and check the Leader's Guide on some easy, inexpensive spiff ideas to get them focused on doing more demos and other activities that generate more sales.

    Complete your action plan and goals on the next page...

Demo Improvement
My Action Page & 90 Day Goal (Continued)

94% of written goals that include a clear plan are achieved.

3. ✍ My 90 day goal: We will improve our demonstration percentage to ____ % of all of our customers and prospects by ___ / ___ / ___.

4. ✍ The steps we'll take to reach our goal on demonstrations are...

  1. _____

  2. _____

  3. _____

  4. _____

✓ Create a 'goals' book for yourself. A simple spiral notebook or 3 ring binder works great.

✓ Get my book, "Goal Setting For Salespeople" for every salesperson and manager. Go to joeverde.com/store. It's free.

✓ Tip: Give each manager a small group of salespeople to train, coach and manage to help each salesperson achieve their individual goals.

5. Hold a short management meeting each morning *just* on your progress on improving demos until you've reached your goal.

"Getting ready is the secret of success."
– Henry Ford

✍ **Write Out Your Thoughts**

_____

_____

_____

_____

_____

_____

_____

_____

_____

_____

_____

_____

_____

_____

_____

_____

_____

_____

_____

_____

_____

_____

_____

"Double down on demos – and you'll double up on sales!"

That's an accurate statement – so write down everything you're
thinking right now about how you can improve demos and sales.

*"Luck is what happens
when preparation meets opportunity."
– Seneca / Circa: 65 AD*

*You have the opportunity to get lucky,
if you'll just make a plan and take action
for every solution we're covering.*

"From just 4 units a <u>month</u>, to 5 the <u>first week</u> with JVTN®..."

"Since we started JVTN®, we've been training every day, both as a group and individually. Before I did anything else, I made it a point to take my new guys aside and practice some of the **basics** with them: we've been working on moving the sale forward by practicing the **greeting** and **bypassing price.**

We're barely one week into the training, and it has already paid off. A new salesperson who's been with me for 3 months sold 4 cars last month. But as of yesterday, he already has 5 on the board for this month, and it's only into week one!

At this rate, his improvement this month alone will cover my store's entire year of JVTN®!"

– Rick Wilson, General Manager
Driver's World, Virginia Beach, Virginia

"I increased my commission $250 per unit!"

"I can't thank my manager enough for sending me to your Sales Workshop. Before the class I was averaging 13.6 cars per month, which isn't bad, but I wanted more and needed a clear plan.

I learned how to **slow** the deal **down** and build more **value**, **stay off price**, and most importantly how to **follow** all of the **8 steps** to the sale (which includes demos).

It definitely worked…I increased my commission by $250 per unit, increased my units as well, and took home a trophy for being in the top 5 salespeople in our group of 11 dealerships.

The timing was perfect because I needed a nice down payment for my new home. Joe, thanks for the tools to make me a sales professional and also for helping make my goal of home ownership a reality!"

– Zach Vogtritter, Salesperson
Springfield Auto Mart, Springfield, Vermont

FLOOR TRAFFIC

SOLUTION #3

RAISE THE GROSS
ON EVERY UNIT YOU SELL

Customers definitely ask price questions and they certainly have price concerns about fitting a new vehicle into their budget. When those questions and concerns are addressed effectively, price falls to the side and isn't anywhere on their list of *most important* concerns when buying a vehicle.

Budget is, and always has been, the real issue when you're working a deal because if they can't come up with the down and they can't afford the payments, there's no deal no matter how much you discount your vehicle.

Price problems come up when those questions and concerns aren't handled correctly on the lot. Then yes, even easy concerns become price objections when salespeople try to close, and those objections will definitely carry over into the negotiation.

Raising the gross *some* is easy. Really raising the gross significantly across the board on every deal is a salesperson and sales management training issue.

Handling price effectively on the lot is great, but the game changes as soon as desking a deal falls back to 'old school' and becomes a price negotiation.

WHICH OF THESE FACTS
AFFECT YOUR PAYCHECK?

✍ *Circle the # for each fact that affects your paycheck...*

1. Buying is *emotional*, negotiation (price discussions) is *logical.* As soon as the conversation moves to price, passion and desire give way to the logic of down, payments, rates, trade values and payoffs. As soon as that happens, the sale gets tougher.

2. 71% buy because they like their salesperson. That's one key reason gross is 40% higher on repeat and referrals than walk-ins.

3. M.I.T. proved the 'like' importance when they found people pay a trusted source 8.1% more. On a $20,000 vehicle, 8.1% translates into $1,620 more – or just about the full asking price.

4. 16% of buyers pay full price & 30% pay what they're asked to pay. Too bad 'full price' isn't what they're asked to pay more often.

5. Price didn't even make the cut in JD Power's Top 10 Buyer survey. Their more important concerns in order were:

    Reliability – Comfort – Styling – Mileage – Quality

    Convenience – Performance – Technology – Image – Safety

6. Price is #16, even when the customer finds a vehicle they want. The first 15 are model, color, equipment and other wants & needs.

7. The average 'first discount' *by a salesperson* within minutes is $844. By the time salespeople start a deal, the average discount is $2,062.

8. 96% who are given what they feel is 'the price' (trade value, etc.) *who are not written up first,* shop the price. That means tossing out a *price hook* on the lot hoping they'll bite is 'sales suicide' 96% of the time.

    The same 96% is true when they feel they've been given 'the price' over the phone or in response to an internet lead.

9. Your Satisfaction Scores are based on how people *feel (emotion).* Customers who paid the highest gross feel better about their purchase and give you the highest Satisfaction Scores, too.

Listen closely – it's salespeople and managers who focus on pricing, not the customer. Most customers just ask a normal, "How much is it?" question. Instead of just answering the question and moving on, salespeople jump into pricing and discounts and never get back to building value.

How To Realistically Improve
Your Net Profit $486,000

Did you know that one of the easiest ways
to increase the net, is to simply raise the gross per unit?

Stop talking price ... After salespeople and managers take our PRICE course on JVTN® or go to class – they're shocked when they get in front of a customer at just *how easy it is to avoid all the price drama,* as they watch their gross (commissions) go through the roof.

No magic here, either. Salespeople need to learn how to manage price *out* of the conversation on the lot, so they can build value and *rephrase* price to budget when they're closing for a commitment, so they can *refocus* price to the 'out of pocket' terms (down & payment) when they're working the deal instead of grinding out the deal on price & trade.

This is so easy because in real life, over
90% of your deals hinge on 'out of pocket' budget.

100	Units delivered now
x $2,500	Average gross per unit now
$250,000	Total gross
x 25%	Increase in gross per unit ($2,500 to $3,175)
$67,500	**Additional Good Gross per month** ($675 x 100)
$810,000	**Additional Good Gross per year**
x 60%	Good Gross to net
$486,000	**Additional Net Profit per year**

Your Cost To Increase Sales & Net Profit ... $1,270

I hope you're seeing that there are plenty of
'Good Gross' opportunities just about everywhere you look.

SKILLS THAT AFFECT GROSS

✍ Circle The Skills That Affect Sales & Gross

*Selling the vehicle and / or raising the gross
involves each of the 3 Core Skills we covered on page 33.*

1. They have to stop thinking *price* is *most* important – it isn't and they have to stop bringing it up even when the customer doesn't.

2. So they can earn a customer's confidence, they have to know how to ask questions to quickly build rapport.

3. They have to ask questions to find each individual's *hot button wants and needs* and select a vehicle based on those hot buttons instead of price.

4. They have to know how to *bypass* price (with questions) to move the conversation away from price and get it back to features and benefits.

5. When they close, they have to ask the right question to *rephrase* price to budget when they do get a price concern or objection.

6. They have to know how to ask questions to demonstrate and present those hot button features instead of just telling people everything they know and how much of a discount they'll get.

7. They have to know how to start the closing process in Step 5 and it's based on a half dozen benefit summary questions.

8. They have to understand *assumptive* closing in Step 6 and they have to master a total of a half dozen 'Either / Or' closing questions.

9. In Step 7 they have to master action closes and know how to get the customer to *take those actions* that equal, "I'm buying this vehicle."

10. The 'silent walk around' of the trade-in is to bring the customer's *hope to get* numbers back to reality, and salespeople have to know how to help them *re-value* their trade without saying a word.

11. They have to know how to ask and get the trade gas mileage, how far the customer drives and if they've spent any money on maintenance so they can use the *gas savings* close and the *maintenance* close in the negotiation to help solve the budget concerns instead of running back and forth dropping the price.

12. Now it's time ... they have to know that final 'Either / Or' final closing question to move inside to start the paperwork.

13. They have to know how to start the negotiation correctly by using the paperwork to get the final, "I know I'm buying this right now" mental commitment the customer has to make to buy the vehicle.

14. They have to know the 4-step, 2-step and zero-step process to turn customers' objections, into deliveries – all by asking the right questions.

15. They have to know the 3-Pass Negotiation process to ask the right questions and respond with the right answers to close the sale.

"Joe, we get all we can – we cannot raise the gross!"

A lot of people really believe it's impossible to raise the gross, they swear they're getting all the money and they won't even consider otherwise.

I understand that – in fact, that's how I felt for years when I struggled with price. Then I learned two things – one, that I could increase the gross *at least some,* and two, I learned how to do it at least some, *almost* every time.

Question ... Can you increase the gross just $5 per unit?

Seriously, on your next deal, could you bump it $5? I'm not talking about a monthly payment that's $5 higher, I'm just talking about charging a total of $5 more than you'd normally take for the vehicle.

"Yeah, but Joe – $5 bucks doesn't matter or prove you can hold more gross." Actually, it does. $5 x 100 units is $500 a mo. / $6,000 a yr. and $3,600 in net profit. Small, yes – worth it? *Yes, from $5 more your net profit jumped by .72%!*

Here's another question: If you can raise gross *anytime* by $5, if your gross is $1,700 now and you increase your average by $5 to get it to $1,705, wouldn't it be true that at that point you could raise it $5 again? (Say 'yes'.)

Do the math – it's scary. Raise the gross $5 per week, and in a year you've raised it $260 per unit. That extra $260 PVR generates $187,200 in net.

Open the 'door of opportunity' just a crack on gross and the sky is the limit.

Try this – when you think your next deal is 'there', tell the salesperson to stick out their hand to shake and say, "My manager said you wouldn't let $10 stand in the way of getting your new car, was he right?" At least half will pay, so you just raised your average $5. Go ahead, try it – it's fun.

Once they get good, switch the question to payment, "My manager said you wouldn't let $10 a month stand in the way, was he right?" ... You'll get half, so $5 x 60 months is $300 / $250 in gross. Holy smokes, that's another $180,000 in additional net profit every year.

Give gross a chance – you'll love it!

OUR POTENTIAL TO RAISE THE GROSS
The Potential You See In Your Dealership

1. ✍ List every salesperson, then in the '+ $_____ per unit' blank, write in how much you feel that person can realistically improve their gross per unit.

   _____ + $_____ per unit   _____ + $_____ per unit

   _____ + $_____ per unit   _____ + $_____ per unit

   _____ + $_____ per unit   _____ + $_____ per unit

   _____ + $_____ per unit   _____ + $_____ per unit

   _____ + $_____ per unit   _____ + $_____ per unit

   _____ + $_____ per unit   _____ + $_____ per unit

   _____ + $_____ per unit   _____ + $_____ per unit

   Total improvement from every salesperson... $ _____ Per Unit

2. ✍ **The Math:** If they had more effective selling skills, could bypass price and build value, and had more confidence working deals...

   a. In #1, we could realistically increase gross by $_____ **per unit**

   b. We currently deliver _____ units per mo.

   c. 'a' x 'b' would add *good gross* of $ _____,_____ per mo.

   d. At 60% of 'c' to net, we'd *net an extra* $ _____,_____ per mo.

   e. In one year, that extra net profit would be $___ , _____ , _____

3. ✍ **WIIFM** (What's in it for me?) If we did a better job of selling and delivered those extra units every month...

   I'd personally earn an extra $ _____ per month,

   and that means I'd make $ _____ more per year.

   The key to selling: Prove the 'value' that the customer wants.

RAISE THE GROSS
My Action Page & 90 Day Goal

1. *Remember...*

Buying Is Not About Price

Buying Is Not About Price

Buying Is Not About Price

2. Did you circle the 'Skills That Affect Gross' in the previous section (on page 54) that you know you can improve, at least some?

3. ✍ My 90 day goal: We will improve our gross per unit by $ _____, by ___ / ___ / ___. (Start small if you need to – it all adds up.)

4. ✍ The steps we'll take to reach our goal on raising the gross are...

    1. _____

       _____

    2. _____

       _____

    3. _____

       _____

    4. _____

       _____

    5. _____

       _____

    ✓ Tip: Give each manager a small group of salespeople to train, coach and manage to help each salesperson achieve their individual goals.

5. Keep the focus on gross *every day.* Hold a short management meeting each morning *just* on your goal and progress on raising the gross until you've reached your goal.

"I went from $29,000 to earning $116,000 to $140,000 per year!"

"Joe – I have been in the car business for 5 years. We started on JVTN® 3 years ago and I have been dedicated to it from day #1.

Some of the things I learned were to **stop pre-qualifying**, to **slow things down** and just **treat everyone as a buyer**. I learned to **handle objections** and to never give up, whether I'm **closing** or **following up** with my customers.

My results have been incredible and in just three years I've gone from making $29,000 per year to $116,000 last year, and I am on track for $140,000 this year.

JVTN® is the most incredible tool for training, and your training is like magic – it's the perfect process for success!"

– Dustin Rudolph, Salesperson
Metro Mitsubishi, Dartmouth, Nova Scotia

That's Some Big Math!

If Dustin's pay went up $111,000 – his dealership's gross also went up 3 to 5 times. Best of all, it was 'good gross' so 60% of that becomes bottom line profit, from just one salesperson.

✍ **Write Out Your Thoughts**

_____
_____
_____
_____
_____
_____
_____
_____
_____
_____
_____
_____
_____
_____
_____
_____
_____
_____
_____
_____
_____
_____
_____
_____

No, you aren't done thinking – we're just getting started.

CHECKLIST

Generating Sales & Good Gross
From The Floor Traffic We Have Now

☑ Salespeople: Improve Selling Skills & Processes

☑ Salespeople: Improve Number Of Demos

☑ Salespeople: Focus Less On Price – More On Value

❑ Management: Work Every Deal / Negotiate For
   More Sales & Maximum Gross

You're improving sales and good gross by improving your salespeople's skills and by getting more people behind the wheel, and you're improving the gross by focusing more on what the customer wants and needs and less on price.

Now let's look at the final step in dealing with customers on the lot – Desking & Negotiation – and let's identify your opportunities for management to improve sales, profits (and customer satisfaction) even more.

FLOOR TRAFFIC
SOLUTION #4

WORKING DEALS
DELIVER MORE UNITS AND
MAXIMIZE THE GROSS

In our Desking & Negotiation class, when we talk about gross profit, we always start by telling everyone not to answer out loud, but just think about this question...

**"Which manager in your dealership
has the lowest gross when they work a deal?"**

Well that never works, because there are usually several managers together in class from each dealership, and people just can't stop themselves from responding *immediately*.

Every time, the manager with the worst gross gets that sheepish grin on his face and lowers his head while all of the other managers from that dealership turn to look at him/her.

We keep it fun, but this is huge when it comes to making or missing more net profit every year, and I'll show you why.

WORKING DEALS FOR
MORE SALES & MAXIMUM GROSS

Add An Extra Month Of Gross Every Year

Why is it that some managers have low gross on deals they work?

• **That's easy, some are better at working deals than others.**

Of course some managers are better at working deals and holding gross than others. No rocket science there – but why?

Maybe it's...

– the process the dealership doesn't have,

– or the process they have, but don't follow,

– maybe it's because they think price is most important, or

– maybe it's about the skills they don't have (yet),

– or it could be a lack of confidence,

– or it could be that they let their salespeople work them harder than they work their customer on each deal,

– or it could just be a bad habit they've developed,

– or maybe it's because no one expects them to improve.

• **Whatever the reason...**

You really do need to do the math on what even one low gross manager who works deals costs you each year.

Here's a hint in that 100 unit dealership:

The lowest grossing manager on deals
may cost as much as...

One full month
of gross profit every year.

HOW TO REALISTICALLY IMPROVE
YOUR NET PROFIT $119,988

One of the easiest ways to increase units and net,
is to work deals for more sales and maximum gross.

Same 100 unit dealership ... $700 in F&I & $1,800 up front.
That means the total monthly front end gross is $180,000.

You'll need to track each manager's deals they work to find each person's average. For this example, let's keep it simple and assume all 3 managers work the same number of deals (33.33) and the lowest gross manager is $500 lower than average.

What does that one low gross manager
working one-third of the deals cost every year?

– $500	**Lower gross per unit compared to the average**
x 33.33	Deals worked each month
– $16,665	In lost *front end* gross per month
– $199,980	**In lost *front end* gross every year**
x 60%	Good gross to net
$119,988	**In additional Net Profit per year**

Your Added Cost ... $2,400

Train that manager to work deals more effectively
in our two workshops on Closing and Negotiation so you can
pick up an **extra $119,988 in net profit** each year.

1. "Closing & Negotiation" for all salespeople and managers
2. "Desking & Negotiation" just for managers

Why both? Because managers have to know exactly how the
vehicle is sold so they can work their deals on budget, not on price.

DESKING & NEGOTIATION POTENTIAL

The Potential You See In Your Dealership

1. ✍ Pull up your gross and units by the manager who worked the deal. Just print the report from your system and you'll see who can improve.

   It's important to always use a 90 day average on all areas you want to improve. Months fluctuate – 3 month rolling averages are your trend, or what we call your 'current average' in that category.

   List the managers who work deals and their *current averages* for front end gross, F&I gross, deals they work and deals they deliver. Then write in your realistic potential if *all managers* improve at least some.

Manager On Deal	Avg. Front	Avg. F&I	Avg. Total	Avg. # Worked	Avg. # Delivered
_____	$ _____	$ _____	$ _____	_____	_____
_____	$ _____	$ _____	$ _____	_____	_____
_____	$ _____	$ _____	$ _____	_____	_____
_____	$ _____	$ _____	$ _____	_____	_____
_____	$ _____	$ _____	$ _____	_____	_____

2. ✍ **The Math:** Seeing the averages by manager in each category above, I think if **all** of our managers improved their Desking & Neg. skills...

   a. We could improve total gross by $_____ **per deal**

   b. Our current average number of deals is   _____ units / mo.

   c. 'a' x 'b' would add *good gross* of $ _____,_____ per mo.

   d. At 60% of 'c' to net, we'd *net an extra* $ _____,_____ per mo.

   e. In one year, that extra net profit would be $___ , _____ , _____

   * For fun, also improve 'units delivered' and do the math there, too.

3. ✍ **WIIFM** (What's in it for me?) If we did a better job of desking and focused more on budget in our negotiations....

   I'd personally earn an extra $ _____ per month,

   and that means I'd make $ _____ more per year.

NEGOTIATION & DESKING

My Action Page & 90 Day Goal

1. Some managers make working deals look so easy and some just don't have it, yet. You need three things to improve sales and gross at the desk...

    *   Clear 'best practice' processes that are effective and repeatable.

    *   Everyone has to develop their skills on working deals with today's buyer.

    *   Consistency – work every deal the same way, every time.

        We teach a very simple 3-pass process that works. Use it every time and you'll increase deliveries and maximize your gross on every deal.

        It works because it addresses and solves all of the issues customers don't like about this last step to buying a vehicle.

        If you don't use our process, that's OK, but you still need a 'best' process, everyone has to develop that skill, and it has to be followed every time.

2. ✍ My 90 day goal: We will improve average gross to $ _____ by working deals more effectively.

3. ✍ The steps we'll take to reach our goal on improving our processes, our skills and our managers who work deals, are...

    1. _____

        _____

    2. _____

        _____

    3. _____

        _____

    ✓ Tip: Create a 'goals' book for yourself. A simple spiral notebook or 3 ring binder works great.

4. Hold a short management meeting each morning to go over everyone's averages on the deals they've worked.

    "Luck is what happens when preparation meets opportunity."
    – Seneca / Circa: 65 AD

An Extra $2,405,988

We just covered *four 'no expense' ways* a 100 unit dealership can **increase net profit from $500,000 per year to $2,905,988 per year** at zero expense with the floor traffic they already have now!

1. Improve Your Selling Skills & Process
2. Demonstrate Vehicles To More Customers
3. Talk Price Less To Increase Gross Profit
4. Improve Your Desking & Negotiation Skills

✍ **List your salespeople and managers
who would improve their results with better skills.**

✍ *List the salespeople & managers who need to improve their **selling skills**...*

_____   _____   _____
_____   _____   _____
_____   _____   _____
_____   _____   _____

✍ *List the salespeople & managers who need to learn to sell value, not **price**...*

_____   _____   _____
_____   _____   _____
_____   _____   _____
_____   _____   _____

✍ *List the managers who need to improve their **desking & negotiation skills**...*

_____   _____   _____
_____   _____   _____

✍ *List the managers who need to improve their **core management skills** so they can train, coach, manage and control their salespeople and their activities more effectively to pick up the extra sales, gross and net profit...*

_____   _____   _____
_____   _____   _____
_____   _____   _____

*Change for growth in business starts from the top down.
Change for growth never starts from the bottom up.*

"I increased my commission $400 per unit!"

"I train on JVTN® and I also recently attended the Closing workshop and WOW! The information and energy I picked up from the workshop truly increased my confidence and my enthusiasm for this business.

Upon learning the **3-pass budget focused negotiation** process, I almost felt it was too easy to go back and ask for all of the money. So I did, and it worked!

I increased my commission per unit by $400 and made more money than ever and had **more customers that liked me** even more!

By focusing on the **value** and getting **more $ down**, I was able to get more deals financed, and was able to deliver more vehicles on shorter terms…which means I would have that customer back that much faster for their next vehicle.

Thanks Joe, for giving us back the secret to having more fun and making more money!"

> *– Omar Vasconez, Salesperson*
> *Ed Bozarth Chevrolet Buick, Grand Junction, Colorado*

✍ *Let's do the math...*

If Omar picked up an extra $400 per unit by **closing on budget** in the negotiation, that's $1,500 to $1,600 per unit for the dealership.

If he's selling 15 units, that's another $20,000–$24,000 in good gross every month – for about $150,000 more net profit per year.

Plus, his customers are happier because he's made their buying experience with him and his dealership **about value, not price.** And they're even happier because his negotiations are focused on helping them fit it into their budget instead of becoming that long, drawn out, back and forth price grind people hate.

Focusing on 'Value' and 'Budget'
totally changes the Negotiation process.

✍ Write Out Your Thoughts

_____

_____

_____

_____

_____

_____

_____

_____

_____

_____

_____

_____

_____

_____

_____

_____

_____

_____

_____

_____

_____

Congratulations – You must have a whole book of great ideas by now!

I take a lot of notes on dozens of topics and keep them in a 3-ring binder. Then depending on the importance, I transfer them to a Word doc in my computer. That way whether they're in the binder or the document, I can keep them by 'subject' and can easily add more notes as I think of them.

Plus, if you'll do the same, you can refer back to your ideas years later when you're looking for a solution to something. You'll be surprised how often you've already solved a problem and have just forgotten.

UNSOLD BUYER FOLLOW UP

SOLUTION #5

Who are your hottest prospects?

Other than people on the lot right now,
your hottest prospect just left without buying.

Four Benefits Of Unsold Follow Up

You've already gone to the expense to put this customer on the lot the first time.

8 out of 10 who leave are still buyers, who'll be buying very soon. When you bring more unsold customers back into your dealership through training and implementing an effective unsold follow up process, you'll ...

1. Sell more units at no extra expense.

2. Increase your "Good Gross" profit.

3. Lower your cost per sale.

4. Increase your net profit.

WHICH OF THESE FACTS
AFFECT YOUR PAYCHECK?

✍ *Circle the # for each fact that affects your paycheck...*

1. 8 out of 10...

    80% were buyers when they came on to your lot, and leaving didn't change that ... 80% of all of those prospects are still buyers and will either buy from you or a competitor.

2. 9 out of 10...

    When people don't buy – 90% of them are not asked for the contact information that's needed to follow up right away.

3. 9 out of 10...

    90% are never contacted again after they leave the dealership.

4. Minutes really do matter...

    People are only stopping at an average of 2 dealerships, so the longer it takes to make the first contact after they leave, the less likely you'll see them again. First contact goal – in 3-5 minutes.

5. 3 out of 9...

    With effective and immediate follow up, 33% (1/3) of the people who leave without buying will come back to your dealership.

6. 2 out of 3...

    67% of the people who do come back into the dealership, buy the vehicle on the spot. That's a 67% closing ratio on be-backs.

7. 9 out of 10...

    You and your salespeople have almost zero competition for this customer because 90% of your competition isn't trained to get contact information and isn't trained or required to follow up.

Fast & Effective Follow Up Is Critical

There just aren't many lookers or shoppers stopping in dealerships today. They did their research before they left the house, and they'll only stop at a couple of dealerships before they buy. To be clear – if they don't buy from you – they do buy from a competitor.

How To Realistically Improve
Sales 67% & Triple Your Net

Here again, dealers don't need more leads to sell more units. In fact, this lead is bought, paid for and didn't buy. Now there's a chance to recoup your investment and earn more 'good gross'.

Here's the math again in that 100 unit dealership...

500	People are on the lot each month
400	Didn't buy, but now through training, SP get...
x 75%	Contact info on everyone who left
300	**Left – *but we got their contact information***
x 33%	Will come back with good follow up
100	People come back in (be-backs)
x 67%	Will buy on their second visit
67	**Sales with unsold follow up**
x $2,500	Average gross per unit
$167,500	Additional Good Gross each month
$2,010,000	**Additional Good Gross per year**
x 60%	Good Gross to Net Profit
$100,500	Additional **Net Profit** per month

+ $1,206,000

Additional **Net Profit** per year

> *Your Cost To Increase Sales & Net Profit ... $1,270*

*If you're on JVTN® take the course on how to follow up
every unsold prospect and then just follow my 6 steps every time.*

UnSold Follow Up Potential
The Potential You See In Your Dealership

1. ✍ List the salespeople who could sell more by improving their selling skills, which by default will improve their unsold follow up skills. Then write in a realistic improvement of the <u>additional units</u> each person could sell with more effective unsold follow up.

   _____ by + ___units   _____ by + ___units

   _____ by + ___units   _____ by + ___units

   _____ by + ___units   _____ by + ___units

   _____ by + ___units   _____ by + ___units

   _____ by + ___units   _____ by + ___units

   _____ by + ___units   _____ by + ___units

   _____ by + ___units   _____ by + ___units

Total improvement from every salesperson... + _____ Units

2. ✍ **The Math:** If we improve their *selling skills* and do a better job of 'unsold follow up', from my estimates above for each person...

a. We could realistically sell   ____ **more units per mo.**

b. Using our total sales and F&I gross of $_____ per unit

c. 'a' x 'b' would add *good gross* of $____,____ per mo.

d. At 60% of 'c' to net, we'd *net an extra* $____,____ per mo.

e. In one year, that extra net profit would be $___ , _____ , _____

3. ✍ **WIIFM** (What's in it for me?) If we taught them to sell and did a better job on 'unsold' and delivered those extra units every month...

    I'd personally earn an extra $ _____ per month,

    and that means I'd make $ _____ more per year.

UnSold Follow Up
My Action Page & 90 Day Goal

1. Easy steps to sell more of your unsold prospects...

    *   Track (count) every person who shows any interest at all in a vehicle. That includes lookers, service customers, kids, etc.

    *   Find *your dealership's* stats: Traffic, demos, sales, and contact info on unsold – contact attempts, appointments, shows, deliveries & gross.

    *   Teach your salespeople to get contact information on everyone.

    *   Start each day with a list of everyone who didn't buy and contact them.

    *   Don't make salespeople's calls for them except when they really can't get them back in. The goal is to teach your salespeople how, so sit down with them regularly as they make their calls. Teach them how first and then make a call or two for them to show them how.

    > *"Tell me and I forget, teach me and I may remember,*
    > *involve me and I learn."* – *Ben Franklin*

2. ✍ My 90 day goal: We will improve our unsold follow up contact percentages from _____ % now to _____ % by ___ / ___ / ___.

3. ✍ The steps we'll take to reach our goal on unsold follow up are...

    1. _____

        _____

    2. _____

        _____

    3. _____

        _____

    ✓ Tip: Give each manager a small group of salespeople to train, coach and manage to help each salesperson achieve their individual goals.

4. Keep the focus on unsold follow up *every day*. Hold a short management meeting each morning *just* on your goal and progress to improve your unsold follow up until you've reached your goal.

"I went from 8 to 15 units. My new goal is 20."

"I have been in the car business 7 months. I started out with an 8-car month, thought I was great, got a little cocky, dropped to 3.

We got JVTN® online training at the dealership and using it helped me understand the **step-by-step process of selling cars** and now I'm averaging 15 units.

The 2-day Sales Workshop I just attended really put everything into perspective and my new goal is to raise my average to 20.

Everyone should attend this class because you really can sell more if you just **follow the basic steps** to the sale."

– Erin Cook, Salesperson
Birchwood Infiniti Nissan, Winnipeg, Manitoba

✍ **Write Out Your Thoughts**

_____

_____

_____

_____

_____

_____

_____

_____

_____

_____

_____

_____

_____

_____

_____

_____

_____

_____

_____

_____

_____

Go back and highlight your 3 most important ideas on unsold follow up.

In your 3-ring binder, add a blank page for each of the 3 key points and start making notes on each of them. Then just like we're doing in here, list who could improve and how, then create an action plan.

When you really get into improving your people, and your sales and gross instead of always trying to buy more sales, this really is fun and profitable.

Quiz

What 3 things do you need for Unsold Customer Follow Up, Incoming Sales Calls, and most Internet Leads to turn each of those contacts into an appointment that will show?

Phone + Selling Skills + A Process

⟶

INCOMING
SALES CALLS

SOLUTION #6

Improve Your Salespeople's
Selling Skills & Your Processes
And Deliver More Units

You don't need more floor traffic to sell more and you don't need more incoming calls or internet leads either. Your salespeople just need better selling skills and a step-by-step process they're required to follow.

It's easy to get these two confused...

Getting *more doesn't equal better* results.

Getting *better equals more* results.

WHICH OF THESE FACTS
AFFECT YOUR PAYCHECK?

✍ *Circle the # for each fact that affects your paycheck...*

1. 9 out of 10 ... 90% of incoming callers buy a vehicle within a week.

2. Your name? ... 75% of incoming callers aren't asked for their name.

3. Your number? ... 85% are not asked for their phone number.

4. Name & Number? ... 93% are not asked for complete contact information – their name *and* their phone number.

5. My name ... On 92% of calls, salespeople don't give them their name.

6. 97% do not schedule an appointment with the customer.

7. No name, no number, no appointment – no surprise...

    88% of incoming callers do not come into the dealership (if they do, it's hard to trace a sale to the incoming call unless the system matches incoming calls and numbers given during the sale).

8. 'Average' stats when incoming calls are handled correctly...

    • 60% appointments

    • 60% of appointments show

    • 50% of appointments that show, buy

9. Critical to understand... *Phone skills are not <u>different</u> skills.*

    The incoming call process (the steps to turn a call into an appointment) is different than the selling process – but the success of every call depends on the person's *selling skills* while they follow the 6 steps of turning a call or internet lead into an appointment that shows.

    Why? Because if a salesperson can't ask the right questions to control the conversation on the lot – they can't on a call either. If they can't bypass price, or rephrase price on the lot - they can't on the phone. If they can't deal with objections, expand their inventory, build rapport or close the sale on the lot – they can't expand inventory, build rapport, and they certainly can't close on a firm appointment that will show.

    *Teach your salespeople how to 'sell', and you'll
    improve sales from your incoming calls and leads by default.*

HOW TO REALISTICALLY INCREASE
SALES 21 UNITS & YOUR NET $378,000

Could You Use A Few More Sales?

Most dealerships don't track incoming sales calls, appointments, shows or deliveries, but that 100 unit dealership gets about 150 sales *calls* each month.

Here's the math on what happens to those incoming calls...

150	Incoming sales calls
x 90%	Will buy within a week
135	Buyers call in each month
– 6	**Sales on average now from incoming sales calls**
129	**Lost sales now from incoming sales calls**

Easy improvement...

27	Sales of 150 calls using avg. stats (#8, p. 78)
= 21	**<u>Additional</u> units per month from incoming calls** (21 additional units + 6 now = 27 total sales)
x $2,500	Average gross per unit
$52,500	Additional Good Gross profit per month
$630,000	More in Good Gross profit per year
x 60%	Good Gross to Net Profit

+ $378,000

Additional **Net Profit** per year

Your Cost To Increase Sales & Net Profit ... $1,270

More good news...you can easily do this by teaching your salespeople their core selling skills and our Incoming Sales Call Process. That means you don't need to add any new departments – so you save even more.

OUR INCOMING CALL POTENTIAL
The Potential You See In Your Dealership

1. ✍ List the salespeople who could sell more by improving their selling skills, which by default will improve their Incoming Sales Call skills. Then write in a realistic improvement of the <u>additional units</u> each person could sell if they could turn more calls into appointments that show.

   _____ by + ___units   _____ by + ___units

   _____ by + ___units   _____ by + ___units

   _____ by + ___units   _____ by + ___units

   _____ by + ___units   _____ by + ___units

   _____ by + ___units   _____ by + ___units

   _____ by + ___units   _____ by + ___units

   _____ by + ___units   _____ by + ___units

   Total improvement from every salesperson... + _____ Units

2. ✍ **The Math:** If we improve their *selling skills* and do a better job on incoming calls, from my estimates above for each person...

   a. We could realistically sell   ____ **more units per mo.**

   b. Using our total sales and F&I gross of $_____ per unit

   c. 'a' x 'b' would add *good gross* of $_____,_____ per mo.

   d. At 60% of 'c' to net, we'd *net an extra* $_____,_____ per mo.

   e. In one year, that extra net profit would be $___ , _____ , _____

3. ✍ **WIIFM** (What's in it for me?) If we did a better job on calls and delivered those extra units every month...

   I'd personally earn an extra $ _____ per month,

   and that means I'd make $ _____ more per year.

INCOMING SALES CALL GOALS
My Action Page & 90 Day Goal

1. These are the *processes* salespeople need to follow to turn more incoming calls or leads into appointments that will show, and the related critical *core selling skills* salespeople need to succeed.

   ✍ *Circle the processes and skills you know they need to improve.*

   a. Process: Rapport Building & Investigation
         Skills: Asking Open Ended & 'Either / Or' Questions
                      Listening – And Expanding The Inventory

   b. Process: Getting Phone Numbers & Names
         Skills: Direct Open Ended Questions

   c. Process: Creating Urgency
         Skills: Mastering Related Urgency Statements
                      Tie-Down & 'Either / Or' Questions

   d. Process: Handling Price Questions
         Skills: Answering & Then Asking A Question
                      Bypassing / Rephrasing Price

   e. Process: Handling Objections: Trade Value / Distance
         Skills: CRIC / 2-Step / 1-Step / Zero-Step
                      Asking The Right Questions

   f. Process: Controlling The Call / Conversation
         Skills: 'Either / Or' Questions

   g. Process: Closing On & Anchoring A Firm Appointment
         Skills: 'Either / Or' & Tie Down Questions

   h. Process: Appointment Verification Prior To Appt.
         Skills: 'Either / Or' Questions
                      Urgency

✓ *Tip from our top Internet Dealers:* Don't send a dozen emails back and forth – instead just pick up the phone and call the number on the lead!

When customers ask about a vehicle, they want a quick response. That's why you're getting fewer internet leads and more incoming calls now.

INCOMING SALES CALLS
My Action Page & 90 Day Goal (Continued)

2. ✍ List each salesperson and the process or skill they need to improve to turn more calls and leads into appointments that show.

Salesperson   Can Improve Process / Skill (# a - h)

_____   _____

_____   _____

_____   _____

_____   _____

_____   _____

_____   _____

_____   _____

_____   _____

_____   _____

3. ✍ My 90 day goal: We will improve our incoming call appointment percentages from _____ % now to _____ % by ___ / ___ / ___.

4. ✍ The steps we'll take to reach our goal on incoming calls are...

1. _____
   _____

2. _____
   _____

3. _____
   _____

4. _____
   _____

✓ Tip: Give each manager a small group of salespeople to train, coach and manage to help each salesperson achieve their individual goals.

5. Keep the focus on incoming calls *every day.* Hold a short management meeting each morning *just* on your goal and progress on improving appointments that show until you've reached your goal.

✍ **Write Down Your Ideas**

Take a few minutes again to think about what you've read
and jot down your ideas now, so you don't misplace them later.

✍ *Other important points for me so far are* _____

_____

_____

_____

_____

_____

_____

_____

_____

_____

✍ *I've also realized* _____

_____

_____

_____

_____

_____

_____

✍ *Besides the goals I've set already, I'll also commit to* _____

_____

_____

_____

_____

_____

"Getting ready is the secret of success."

– Henry Ford

"I went from 88 units last year, to almost 200 this year."

"I recently returned from your Sales Workshop and all I can say is WOW, what an eye opener!

In your class, I learned the importance of **slowing down** the sale, being a **better listener** and asking the **right questions** to build **more value** in myself, my product and the dealership.

The results: 2 months ago I sold 13 units, and last month I was the top salesperson with 21 units and great gross!

Last year, I sold 88 cars and averaged about 7.5 units per month. It's only the middle of June and I've already sold 77 units for the year, I'm averaging 15.4 units per month now and that puts me on track for almost 200 units this year.

Joe – thanks for showing me **the path to success** and for providing the tools it takes to get there!"

– Paul Poltz, Salesperson
Goss Dodge Chrysler Inc., South Burlington, Vermont

DAILY PROSPECTING

SOLUTION #7

Generate New Business
Through Daily Prospecting

You hired salespeople to do 3 things...

1. **Sell** the vehicle once they're with a customer.

2. **Retain** the customers they sell long-term to become service and parts customers, and future sales.

3. **Develop** their own business through daily prospecting in service, by phone, by mail or email, and also by prospecting in person.

    Note: When we teach prospecting, we only focus on finding the next buyer in the family. And we do that just by talking to people who already know us, or who are already customers of the dealership.

    There's never a need to sit salespeople down to make cold calls to strangers to try to get them to buy a car.

WHICH OF THESE FACTS
AFFECT YOUR PAYCHECK?

✍ *Circle the # for each fact that affects your paycheck...*

1. 95% of the people either own a vehicle now or will be getting one.

2. 71% bought because they liked the salesperson they worked with.

3. 30% *of all of the people* have a family member who'll be buying a vehicle within 90 days. These are Hot Prospects.

    Note: 'All' includes *all* of your family and friends, *all* service and parts customers, *all* of your previous customers, *all* of the customers in the dealership's CRM / DMS, and *everyone else. All* means *ALL.*

4. 62% know someone who'll be buying within 90 days.

5. 63% have no intention of buying their next vehicle from the same salesperson or dealership where they bought their last vehicle. That's no surprise because...
    *   90% were never contacted about buying another vehicle.
    *   82% can't remember their last salesperson's name a year later.

6. Deliver 3 out of 4. The average closing ratio on a repeat customer or prospect a salesperson or manager brings into the dealership is 75%.

7. Big $$$ ... The average gross on a repeat customer, referral or the prospect a salesperson or manager brings into the dealership is 40% higher than the average gross on any type of walk-in prospect.

8. Big Savings ... Not only do they pay 40% more gross, each repeat or referral sale you make saves you another $500 or so, compared to an ad-driven or purchased lead-driven sale.

9. More Great News ... The average family will purchase 36 vehicles.

10. No Competition ... The average dealership sells 75%–80% of their vehicles to expensive, ad-driven, price-shopping, tough to close, lower gross prospects – and only 20% to 25% to easy to close, higher grossing repeat customers, referrals and prospects.

------- TIP --------

Stop working so hard and spending so much money to get *high cost, low gross* customers you close at 20% (at best). Work smart instead & get more *low cost, high gross* prospects who buy 75% of the time & pay you 40% more gross.

UNLIMITED OPPORTUNITY

Prospecting isn't just a Gold Nugget – It's a Gold Mine!

This is the hardest group to put an improvement number on,
because your potential is only limited by your commitment.

Prospecting offers so much opportunity for growth that you could literally stop all advertising, put a chain link fence around your dealership, and only sell to repeat customers, their referrals, to current dealership customers in parts and service, and to prospects your salespeople and managers bring into the dealership ... *and you'd double your sales and increase your net by 943%.*

Imagine going from an *expensive, ad-driven* 100 units with 10 salespeople and a $500,000 net, to a 200 unit dealership with only 10 salespeople (and 2 or 3 sales assistants) who drive their own business with just these groups, at a $5,200,000 net instead? (Use the calculator at JoeVerde.com/netcalc)

Imagine the fun, the growth, the profit and the income for everyone that would be generated with 80% of your sales coming from high profit, low cost, easy to close, friendly people – instead of ad-driven price shoppers.

How many Hot Prospects are there *per month* in a 100 unit dealership that's been in business 10 years?

500	Customers in service every month
x 30%	Have a family member buying within 90 days
150	**Hot Prospects In Service**

12,000	Previous customers in the CRM (10 years x 1,200 yr.)
x 30%	Family member trading in 90 days
3,600	**Hot Prospects In The CRM / DMS**

✍ Do the math for your dealership.
How many Hot Prospects do you have each month?

We have	_____	Customers in our **service** department every month
We have	_____	Previous customers and others in our **database**
Total:	_____	**Customers to prospect *in our dealership* each month**
	x 30%	Have a family member who will buy within 90 days
We have	_____	**Hot prospects who'll buy within 90 days, if not from us, from a competitor.** (We'd prefer they buy from us.)

Prospecting Opportunity

Let's look at the results you could expect from some realistic daily prospecting in that typical 100 unit dealership...

Average salespeople have almost 6 hours of down time each day and considering that very large unused block of time, I've used a *very low, very realistic number of prospecting contacts (below)*.

You can easily double this number of contacts – at least until the contacts start to create so much new floor traffic, that salespeople are actually working most of their shift instead of waiting for your dealership to supply them with more expensive, price shopping, harder to close, low gross, walk-in customers.

Question: How long does a 5 minute prospecting call take?
Exactly, somewhere around 5 minutes – so keep that in mind and do the math before you say they don't have time to make these contacts.

1. **Prospecting Out In Your Service Drive**

   Being realistic, let's have each salesperson talk to *just 1 customer* in service each day and use the 5 question referral / prospecting script.

250	Contacts per mo. (10 SP @ 1 each x 25 days)
x 30%	Family member trading in 90 days
75	**Hot Prospects In Service Each Month**

2. **Prospecting In Your Existing Sold Customers Database**

   In 6 hours of down time, at 5 minutes per call, a salesperson could make 72 outgoing calls every day. But let's don't even go there.

   So being realistic – let's have each salesperson call *just 10* sold customers or anyone else in your CRM / DMS using the 5 question referral script.

2,500	Contacts per mo. (10 SP @ 10 calls ea. x 25 days)
x 30%	Family member trading in 90 days
750	**Hot Prospects In Your Own Database**

Total ... <u>825 More Hot Prospects</u> Per Month!

How To Realistically Increase Sales
149 Units & Earn 6x Your Net

With 825 hot prospects per month from 10 salespeople
making just 10 calls each and just 1 service contact per day.

What is the <u>realistic</u> low potential in a 100 unit dealership?

825	Hot prospects
x 60%	Appointments (this will be closer to 70-80%)
495	Appointments made
x 60%	Will show (this will be closer to 70-80%)
297	Appointments show
x 50%	Will buy (this will be closer to 60-70%)
149	Deliveries
x $2,500	Average gross per unit
$372,500	**Additional gross monthly from prospecting**
x 12	Months
$4,470,000	Additional 'good gross' each year

Your Annual Net Profit Improvement

x 60%   Good Gross to Net Profit

$2,682,000 Additional Net Profit

Too high? Cut it in half – you'd still have...

$1,341,000 Additional Net Profit

Still too high? Cut it in half again
and you've still added ...

$670,500 In Additional Net Profit

(Your cost: $1,270)

With $2.6 million realistically at stake from prospecting, remind me again...
Why spend $500,000 a year to run price ads instead of teaching salespeople and
managers how to control your dealership's sales, growth and profit each year?

OUR PROSPECTING POTENTIAL

The Potential You See

1. ✍ List the salespeople who can do a better job of prospecting by improving their selling skills and write their realistic improvement.

   Yep, it's still all about "selling skills" (asking the right questions in the right order, at the right time) to bring in more of their own prospects with 40% higher gross profit and zero selling expense into the dealership.

   _____ by + ___units   _____ by + ___units

   _____ by + ___units   _____ by + ___units

   _____ by + ___units   _____ by + ___units

   _____ by + ___units   _____ by + ___units

   _____ by + ___units   _____ by + ___units

   _____ by + ___units   _____ by + ___units

   Total improvement from every salesperson...   + _____ Units

2. ✍ **The Math:** If each of our salespeople developed more effective selling skills and prospected each day, I think...

   a. We could realistically sell   _____ **more units per mo.**

   b. Using our total sales and F&I gross of $_____ per unit

   c. 'a' x 'b' would add *good gross* of $_____,_____ per mo.

   d. At 60% of 'c' to net, we'd *net an extra* $_____,_____ per mo.

   e. In one year, that extra net profit would be $___ , _____ , _____

3. ✍ **WIIFM** (What's in it for me?) If we did a better job of prospecting every day and delivered those extra units every month...

   I'd personally earn an extra $ _____ per month,

   and that means I'd make $ _____ more per year.

PROSPECTING GOALS
My Action Page & 90 Day Goal

1. Prospecting to find the next buyer in a family is very easy. Ask the right 5 questions at the right time and you'll end up finding the next buyer in the family almost every time. And 30% of the time, you'll also have a hot prospect who'll be buying within 90 days.

Process: Ask 5 Questions In The Proper Order...

• 3 Open Ended Questions

• 2 'Either / Or' Questions

Skills: Know The Correct Questions To Ask

2. ✍ My 90 day goal: We will improve our deliveries each month from daily prospecting from just ___ or ___ per month now to a minimum of ____ per month by ___ / ___ / ___.

3. ✍ The steps we'll take to reach our goal on prospecting are...

   1. _____

   _____

   2. _____

   _____

   3. _____

   _____

   4. _____

   _____

   ✓ Tip: Give each manager a small group of salespeople to train, coach and manage to help each salesperson achieve their individual goals.

4. Keep the focus on prospecting *every day.* Hold a short management meeting each morning *just* on your goal and progress on prospecting until you've reached your goal.

✍ Write Out Your Thoughts

_____

_____

_____

_____

_____

_____

_____

_____

_____

_____

_____

_____

_____

_____

_____

_____

_____

"I feel like I'm getting my degree in sales."

"I have been training on JVTN® for one year and love it. There's nothing better to keep you focused and on track every day!

After attending the Sales Workshop, too, and covering so much in two days, it pulled everything I'd learned on JVTN® together.

After class, I focused on **staying off price, slowing** the sale **down** and **building** the **value** by **asking** the right **questions.**

I normally average 11.5 per month and after class I sold 19 in April, and 16 in May! Thanks Joe, with JVTN® and your classes, I feel like I'm getting **my degree in sales!"**

– Taylor Robbins, Salesperson
North Country Auto, Presque Isle, Maine

Why Focus On A Solution For 90 Days?

One of the biggest problems with improvement is management trying to keep the focus on the improvement long enough for it to stick.

Take doing more demos for example – you could put a $10 spiff on them for 30 days and double demos. You'd sell a bunch of extra units, do high fives with everyone, and too many assume improving demos is done, so they take on the next solution; unsold follow up or holding gross.

As soon as the focus on demos is lifted, what happens? Absolutely, the improvement quickly slides back to its previous level. That's why you hear so many managers who only focused on a change for a month say, "Oh, we did that and it worked for awhile, but it didn't stick."

The goal is to develop a new habit – so how long does that take?

The last stat I read said 64 days to make it *stick*. In class, we always recommend you give every change 60 to 90 days of continuous focus, because the real goal is making every new change just part of how you do business. That starts with implementing your new process / new rule...

New Rule → Habit → Managed Habit → Philosophy / Values

When you first make a change, implement a process, it becomes a new rule. Problem is, people don't like change or new rules so they resist. That's why you have to focus on any new change daily for 60-90 days or more to get past the band of resistance fighters and develop a new habit.

But wait, you can't walk away from your focus on that change even after 90 days or it will gradually start dropping again. So while you take on your next new solution and start training, you still have to continue to manage / touch previous processes daily, too.

So 60-90 days of process, rule, daily management, and another 60-90 days of focus as you move to the next solution. Now as long as you always hold the line on the skills, habits and process in that solution, within 6 months it becomes just part of how you do business; your philosophy / your values.

That's critical because when you hire new salespeople, they'll learn the rules and boundaries in your dealership from what everyone else does, not from what you put into your procedure manual.

When everyone follows the steps to selling, gives great demos, focuses on value, follows up when they miss a sale, handles calls correctly, and prospects daily – that's what your new guy does, too.

The goal isn't to just 'try something new' with these solutions,
the goal is to implement processes to improve how you do business.

Congratulations Brandon!

"Half a million per month..."

*"From 130 units @ $2,700 per unit
to 239 units @ $4,100 per unit with Joe's training."*

"I started as a salesman at a Dodge store with no experience in the car business and came to Joe Verde training before I did anything else.

My third month, I became salesman of the month and then salesman of the year. My dealership was the #1 in the nation and I pride myself on being the #1 salesperson at the #1 dealership.

I moved to Texas to be closer to family and went to work at the Dodge dealership. I was salesman of the month my first two months and they'd never seen anything like the Joe Verde processes.

They didn't know the steps to the sale, they didn't know how to stay off price, or how to sell the car. So they promoted me to manager and at 25, I was the youngest manager the store had ever had.

I hold training Monday through Friday from 10:15 to 11:15 every morning. We cover Joe's steps, or closes or whatever else we need to focus on that day.

When I started training, the store was doing 130 units per month at $2,700 per copy. Last month we did 239 at about $4,100 each.

*That's 100 more units and way over
a half a million improvement in gross every month.*

The guys have improved, the store has improved and it's from Joe Verde training every single day!

Thank you Joe, I attribute everything to your training and I am your biggest advocate."

*– Brandon Bourke,
General Sales Manager, Dodge, Texas*

Talk about a win / win, read his story again slowly.
This is how you can increase good gross profit by
$500,000 or more every month in your dealership.

YOUR DEALERSHIP'S POTENTIAL

THE BIG MATH

Numbers – Numbers – Numbers

We tossed around a lot of numbers to see what's going on now, and the great opportunity you have in each of the solutions we covered.

Now it's your turn to put a number and dollar figure on the opportunities *you believe you found to improve* your units, your good gross and the net profit in your dealership.

Why don't most people ✍ fill in the blanks?

*A Dealer <u>who did fill in all of the blanks</u>
said it in class – and said it better than I ever could...*

He said that when I say something or toss out a stat or number, *maybe it's true* and then again, *maybe it isn't* for his store. He said that possibility alone makes it real easy for anyone to ignore what we've covered and justify doing nothing differently tomorrow than they did yesterday.

Then he said when *he* fills in the blanks, that number or solution and the potential become *true for him, his managers and his dealership,* and makes it impossible for them to say they want to grow and improve and then not make the changes they agree they can and need to make, to improve.

I agree, and I also know it's partly because a lot of people assume that if they honestly *think* about it, that's enough. Unfortunately, that's also how 87% of the people set goals and why they don't hit 97% of them. You have to *write out* your goals and your plans to hit them. It's the same with potential, you have to *write it out* to internalize the impact these changes will have.

So if you haven't already, go back and fill in the blanks. It'll be great to really get a clear picture of what you feel is your real potential. Plus I guarantee you'll have lots to talk about in your next management meeting.

And if you're unsure it's worth it, go home and say, "Honey, I learned today that I could earn twice as much as I'm making now, do it easier, and in less time so we could have more, do more and so that I could spend more time with you – what do you think, should I do it?"

Seriously now! Just follow the steps on the next two pages...

YOUR BIG MATH

✍ Just fill in the potential you see in each solution.

1. Improve Your Salespeople's Core Selling Skills

   a. Unit Improvement Per Month   _____ units per mo.

   b. Good Gross Profit Per Month $ ____, _____, _____ mo.

   c. Net Improvement Per Year $ ____, _____, _____ yr.

2. Increase The Number Of Demos To Your Customers

   a. Unit Improvement Per Month   _____ units per mo.

   b. Good Gross Profit Per Month $ ____, _____, _____ mo.

   c. Net Improvement Per Year $ ____, _____, _____ yr.

3. Improve Your Overall Gross Per Unit

   a. Unit Improvement Per Month   __N/A__ units per mo.

   b. Good Gross Profit Per Month $ ____, _____, _____ mo.

   c. Net Improvement Per Year $ ____, _____, _____ yr.

4. Sell More Units & Improve Your Lowest Gross With More Effective Desking & Negotiation Skills & Processes

   a. Unit Improvement Per Month   _____ units per mo.

   b. Good Gross Profit Per Month $ ____, _____, _____ mo.

   c. Net Improvement Per Year $ ____, _____, _____ yr.

5. Improve Your Unsold Follow Up

   a. Unit Improvement Per Month   _____ units per mo.

   b. Good Gross Profit Per Month $ ____, _____, _____ mo.

   c. Net Improvement Per Year $ ____, _____, _____ yr.

YOUR BIG MATH

You don't need to do everything all at once,
just start with what's most important to you & take it from there.

6. Improve Your Sales From Incoming Calls & Leads

   a. Unit Improvement Per Month   _____ units per mo.

   b. Good Gross Profit Per Month $ ____, _____, _____ mo.

   c. Net Improvement Per Year $ ____, _____, _____ yr.

7. Improve Your Daily Prospecting In Service & To Your Database

   a. Unit Improvement Per Month   _____ units per mo.

   b. Good Gross Profit Per Month $ ____, _____, _____ mo.

   c. Net Improvement Per Year $ ____, _____, _____ yr.

NOW FIND YOUR TOTAL IMPROVEMENT POTENTIAL

a. Your <u>Unit</u> Potential (1a - 7a)

   We'd Deliver An Additional _____ Units Per Mo.

   We'd Deliver An Additional _____ Units Per Yr.

b. Your <u>Good Gross</u> Profit Potential (1b - 7b)

   We'd Generate $ ____, _____, _____ In Addl. Good Gross Per Mo.

   We'd Generate $ ____, _____, _____ In Addl. Good Gross Per Yr.

c. Your <u>Net Profit</u> Potential (1c - 7c)

   We'd Generate $ ____, _____, _____ In Addl. Net Profit Per Mo.

   We'd Generate $ ____, _____, _____ In Addl. Net Profit Per Yr.

d. WIIFM: From the increases above in units and net profit...

   I'd personally earn an extra $ _____ per month,

   and that means I'd make $ _____ more per year.

> # $7,096,980
> The realistic gross profit potential
> every year in a 100 unit dealership.

How's that for some quick and easy volume and profit!

Will you get all of the sales and profit we outlined? Probably not, but with all of the potential we talked about, you can definitely improve, right now, just by picking one solution and focusing on it.

As you learn to work those good gross sources, you'll quickly find you never go back to asking those, "What's the budget" questions, or saying, "Let's give up some gross this weekend so we can sell more."

Instead of focusing on ads and compromises to try to sell more, you'll find that you start asking yourself questions like those below about these high value, high probability solutions to make those extra sales.

• What's our percentage of write ups to traffic? How about deliveries to write ups? Who can improve, so we can improve sales & good gross?

• What's our demo ratio? Who needs to do more? What's the plan?

• How are our managers doing working deals – are we sticking to 'budget focused negotiations' or have we slipped back into 'price focused'?

• What about gross – are we giving our customers the chance to pay more by building value? Who has the lowest gross, so we improve it?

• What about prospecting out in service and on the phone – how are we doing with that, who can improve, which manager can help?

• What's our status on incoming calls and leads – how are we doing turning them into appointments that show? Where can we improve?

• Are we getting contact info on our unsold prospects ? What percent are we getting back on the lot for another chance to make the sale?

Now instead of just hoping an ad will work, you have 7 solutions you can implement any time that will increase units, gross and net profit.

How will you know what to focus on?

Start tracking everything in sales using the VSA® in JVTN®. When you do, the information you'll gather will point right to the solution you need to focus on right then, that day, to increase sales and profits.

There's so much more to learn...

There are so many other things to learn that we just don't pick up through the daily experiences in management that will help you save time, money and frustration when you want to sell more, so do this...

1. Get my 'Goals' book for every salesperson and manager ... it's on exactly how to set and reach sales goals, and how to manage your current averages in every area we covered to push continuous growth. It's free.

2. Get my 'Recovery & Growth' book for the dealer and every manager. This book generates the most 'Holy smokes, I never realized that!' on what you *must* do in management to continually grow. It's free.

3. If you're on JVTN® now, use the VSA® tracking included. The 'Virtual Sales Assistant' is exactly that, and you'll always have live, up to the minute answers to any of those 7 questions on, 'How can we sell more now?'

4. If you aren't on JVTN®, sign up now and make one commitment – to *follow my directions on which 4 courses to cover first* – you'll see more enthusiasm, confidence and results than you ever imagined possible.

   Within 30 days, get one manager to our Team Leadership class, and one to our Train the Trainer workshop on how to hold great training in your dealership. Both classes are included with full subscriptions to JVTN®.

5. If you haven't been to our 2-Day Team Leadership class for dealers and managers, *cancel whatever you've planned for next week and sign up now.* 99.9% of the dealers and managers who've attended said you should get to this class right now. Why? Because *experience* didn't teach us the most important keys to success in management, and that's what we cover in that 2-Day class.

6. Optional – Very Fast Start ... You and another manager bring two of your salespeople to our 2-Day Sales workshop, so you understand how easy it is to develop high achievers, and so your salespeople understand how easy it is to become high achievers in sales.

Become 'Management Driven' Not 'Market Dependent'

A foundation to continuous growth is *becoming* management driven instead of being an advertising / price / market dependent dealership.

When you do the things we've covered, you become 'management driven' by default, and that means you'll never have to worry about having a great economy or perfect weather to turn a profit.

Congratulations! Enjoy your success, and please let us know about your results.

"When you can see it and believe it, you can achieve it." – Napoleon Hill

Can you see your gold mine?

If You See Your Potential – It's Time To Take Action

We've uncovered 7 great opportunities just sitting on your lot waiting to become sales, gross profit and net profit. And there's really only one catch: Just like digging for gold in a mine, your managers and salespeople have to have the right tools to do the job, or it can't happen.

Most dealers keep trying to hire or advertise their way to more success, hoping the next gold miner they hire will be better equipped than the last. For most, it's become a repeating cycle with no end in sight.

There is a solution and *when you're ready to go for your gold,* we offer the best training on the planet for salespeople and managers in the car business. So when you're ready to take your dealership to *the next level,* we have all of the processes, training and tools to help you get there.

Circle the opportunity you plan to focus on first...

Then call us and we'll help you select the training solution
that will be best for your dealership to target your specific goals.

#1 Improving Selling Skills – To Improve Closing & Delivery Ratios

#2 Improving Demos – To Deliver More Units & Improve Gross

#3 Increasing Gross – By Effectively Managing Price & Building Value

Joe Verde Solutions For Your Salespeople & Managers

- 2-Day Workshop....How To Sell A Car Today

- 2-Day Workshop....Advanced Closing, Objections, Handling Price, Setting Up Budget-Focused Negotiation

- JVTN® Courses......Ask The Right Questions & Close More Sales
  PRICE – Managing Price In Every Situation
  How To Sell More Cars – The Selling Process
  The Basics Of Closing The Sale
  20+ Ways To Close The Sale
  The Basics Of Handling Objections
  The Basics Of (Budget-Focused) Negotiating
  Closing In The Negotiation

#4 Desking & Negotiation: Improving Sales & Gross With A More Effective Budget-Focused Process and Desking Skills
- 2-Day Workshop   Desking & Negotiation (For Managers Only)
- 2-Day Workshop   How To Sell A Car Today
- 2-Day Workshop   Advanced Closing, Objections, Price, Negotiation
- JVTN® Courses   The Basics Of Handling Objections
                   The Basics Of (Budget-Focused) Negotiating

#5 Improving Sales Through Unsold Follow Up
- 2-Day Workshop   Business Development
- JVTN® Course   Turn Unsold Customers Into Be-Backs & Deliveries

#6 Improving Sales From Incoming Calls & Internet Leads
- 2-Day Workshop   Business Development
- JVTN® Course   Turn Calls & Leads Into Appointments That Show

#7 Improving Sales & Profit Through Daily Prospecting
- 2-Day Workshop   Business Development
- JVTN® Course   Prospecting For New Business

Three Critical 2-Day Courses For Every Manager
These are the three most important courses your managers have never been to, because they aren't taught by anyone but us.

- Team Leadership ... Most managers were hired or promoted with no real training on the potential or the critical responsibilities and requirements it takes to manage and develop high achievers in sales. This is *the most important* workshop they've never attended.

- Desking & Budget-Focused Negotiation ... In the last step in buying, customers today want a quick & easy process, no grind. You can do that with our simple "3-Pass Negotiation" process and focus on budget, not on price. Attend this class and deliver more units, maximize your gross profit on every deal and improve your CSI overnight.

- Training Your Trainer ... Continued growth requires continuous improvement. For that to happen, every manager has to know how to turn sales meetings into effective training sessions, and then train, coach, and continually develop your salespeople to new, higher levels.

Isn't it time to try a new approach to profit and growth? Training is the only permanent solution for both, so call us today.

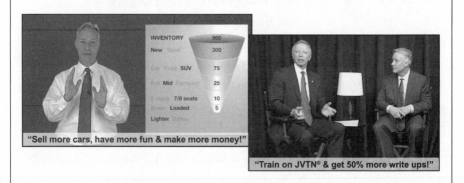

JOE VERDE SALES WORKSHOPS

Workshop #1	Workshop #2	Workshop #3
How To Sell A Car & Close The Sale	How To Close The Sale, Overcome Objections And Negotiate	Business Development Internet / Phone
Aren't you tired of explaining why you don't sell more? Sign up now.	Get solid buying commitments, more deliveries & higher gross.	You're only missing 8 out of 9 deliveries from your lead sources. We fix that.

"My sales exploded to 20 units."

"When I started in the car business, I immediately started training on JVTN®.

My first month, I sold 8 units and then I went to Joe's 2 Day Sales Workshop. WOW, talk about a pump up!

I came back ready to follow his steps to the sale, slowed down and focused on building value. I got a quick hat trick and never looked back – my sales exploded to 20 for the month."

– Ian Daly, Salesperson
Ruge's Chrysler Dodge Jeep, NY

Double Your Sales!
Call Today
(888) 595-5610

"Sell more cars, have more fun and make more money!"

Questions? Call Now (888) 595-5610

JOE VERDE MANAGEMENT & SALES TOOLS

Make Record Sales – Get Joe's 2 Monthly Newsletters

• **Selling Cars Today** – Salespeople need new and updated information every day. Use Joe's easy to read, monthly newsletters for your daily training. Each month, they're filled with winning sales strategies guaranteed to keep your salespeople on track and moving toward the winner's circle every day.

• **For Sales Managers Only** – The only monthly newsletter written just for Sales Managers. With new information to help you hire, manage and train your sales team for success in today's new market.

Newsletters are available both online or in print.

Books For Salespeople
Get copies for everyone today!

• **Manage Your Career In Sales: Goal Setting for Salespeople**

Are you ready to get what you want in sales? If you're serious about taking your career to the next level, Joe's book will show you how to totally control your sales and income every month and every year.
Get your printed copy (shipping rates apply) or get your free PDF download today!

• **Earn Over $100,000 Selling Cars – Every Year**
Your potential selling cars is incredible. You can get lucky and make $10,000 in one month. But you won't get lucky enough to make over $100,000 every year – that takes skills and a plan.
Get your printed copy (shipping rates apply) or download your free PDF today!

• **How To Sell A Car Today**
Close almost 50% of the people you talk to if you follow the "Steps To Selling" in this book 100% of the time, with all of your prospects. Let's take your sales, income and career to your next level.

• **38 Hot Tips**
Here's an easy way to increase your sales right now! Inside are 38 great ideas on how to sell more cars in today's market and answers to common sales questions.

Plan For Your Success

• *Plan Your Day, Plan Your Week!*
Weekly Pocket Guides

The hidden problem is daily activity management. Make it easy with this on the lot pocket-size weekly planner for your salespeople.

• *Plan Your Month!*
Monthly Planning Guides

For Sales: Set goals, measure your performance, create your plan & increase your income!

For Managers: The easy way to track, forecast, set goals and follow up with your sales team.

For Dealers Only

A Dealer's Guide To Recovery & Growth

Get the book that will change your life with a common sense, step-by-step process you can follow to grow your dealership. If you're struggling, follow these steps and be profitable in 30 days. If you're making money, follow these steps to double or triple your net profit. Available for print and free download at JoeVerde.com.

Don't Miss Another Sale – Call Now (888) 595-5610

✍ My 'To Do' List

"The one word that makes a good manager – decisiveness."

"The speed of the boss is the speed of the team."

– Lee Iacocca

✍ My 'To Do' List

_____

_____

_____

_____

_____

_____

_____

_____

_____

_____

_____

_____

_____

_____

_____

_____

_____

_____

_____

_____

_____

_____

"If you think you can do a thing or
think you can't do a thing, you're right."
– Henry Ford